FOOTBALL ⬤ SUPERSTARS

# Peyton Manning

# FOOTBALL SUPERSTARS

*Tiki Barber*

*Tom Brady*

*John Elway*

*Brett Favre*

*Peyton Manning*

*Dan Marino*

*Donovan McNabb*

*Joe Montana*

*Walter Payton*

*Jerry Rice*

*Ben Roethlisberger*

*Barry Sanders*

FOOTBALL ★ SUPERSTARS

# Peyton Manning

Samuel Willard Crompton

✅® Checkmark Books™
*An imprint of Facts On File, Inc.*

## PEYTON MANNING

Copyright © 2008 by Infobase Publishing

Checkmark Books
An imprint of Infobase Publishing
132 West 31st Street
New York NY 10001

**Library of Congress Cataloging-in-Publication Data**
Crompton, Samuel Willard.
  Peyton Manning / Samuel Willard Crompton.
      p. cm. — (Football superstars)
  Includes bibliographical references and index.
  ISBN 978-0-7910-9605-5 (hardcover)
  ISBN 978-1-60413-322-6 (paperback)
  1. Manning, Peyton. 2. Football players—United States—Biography—Juvenile literature.
  3. Quarterbacks (Football)—United States—Biography—Juvenile literature. I. Title.
  II. Series.

  GV939.M289C76 2008
  796.332092—dc22
  [B]
                        2007040952

Checkmark Books are available at special discounts when purchased in bulk quantities for businesses, associations, institutions, or sales promotions. Please call our Special Sales Department in New York at (212) 967-8800 or (800) 322-8755.

You can find Chelsea House on the World Wide Web at http://www.chelseahouse.com

Text design by Erik Lindstrom
Cover design by Ben Peterson

Printed in the United States of America

Bang EJB 10 9 8 7 6 5 4 3 2 1

This book is printed on acid-free paper.

All links and Web addresses were checked and verified to be correct at the time of publication. Because of the dynamic nature of the Web, some addresses and links may have changed since publication and may no longer be valid.

# CONTENTS

# Battling Brothers

**W**hile the national anthem was playing in the background, the older brother kept looking over at the younger one. "I was thinking how proud I am that he's my little brother," Peyton Manning told the *New York Times*. It was September 10, 2006, and the first Sunday night game of the **National Football League (NFL)** season was about to be played. Taking place at Giants Stadium, which serves as the home field for both the New York Giants and the New York Jets, the game featured the first matchup in NFL history between brothers who were the starting **quarterbacks** for their respective teams.

### ELI AND PEYTON

Thirty-year-old Peyton Manning was very much the star of the show. Starting his ninth season with the Indianapolis Colts, he had already broken many NFL records. The most impressive was **touchdown** passes in a season: In 2004, he had thrown 49 of them, breaking the previous record held by one of his boyhood heroes, former Miami Dolphins quarterback Dan Marino. In September 2006, Peyton Manning stood atop the football world in terms of individual accomplishments, but he had yet to win a Super Bowl, the crowning achievement that defines the greatness of many quarterbacks in the NFL.

Twenty-five-year-old Eli Manning (his full name is Elisha) was also a starting NFL quarterback, but he had a long way to go to attain the star status achieved by his elder brother. Eli had attended the University of Mississippi, where he had started at quarterback for three years. In the 2004 NFL draft, he was selected by the New York Giants as the first overall pick. During the first nine games of his rookie season, he was the understudy to Kurt Warner, but in Week 11, he earned his first start against the Atlanta Falcons. The following year, Eli was named the **starter** from the get-go and led the Giants in every game that season. He threw for six touchdowns and 1,043 **yards** his first season but then came into his own in 2005, passing for 3,762 yards and 24 touchdowns. Most astute football observers believed that Peyton had the better arm and was more accurate, but most experts also agreed that Eli had a good upside. Although he was much quieter than his older brother, Eli was not going to back down when the two squared off against each other. The *New York Times* put it this way:

> As the two played against each other for the first time, becoming the first siblings in NFL history to start as opposing quarterbacks, the little brother was every bit his more accomplished older brother's equal.

Peyton's team, the Indianapolis Colts, started off well. On the first possession, he led a 17-play, 58-yard **drive** to the Giants' 9-yard line, where newly acquired kicker Adam

Vinatieri booted a 26-yard **field goal**. (Before the Colts signed him as a free agent from New England in March 2006, Vinatieri was a thorn in their side; in the 2003 **American Football Conference (AFC)** Championship Game, he kicked five field goals in the Patriots' 24-14 win against the Colts.)

Well aware that they were facing the quarterback with the best numbers in the NFL, the Giants chose not to make it a battle between Eli and Peyton—at least not to start. Instead, they relied on **running back** Tiki Barber, a 10-year veteran who was coming off a stellar season in which he finished second in the NFL with 1,860 yards rushing. During their first two drives, the Giants moved the ball better than the Colts, but they were thwarted both times, while the Colts built up a 13-0 lead thanks to 26- and 32-yard field goals by Vinatieri and a two-yard touchdown pass from Peyton Manning to **tight end** Dallas Clark. Fortunately, for the Giants, Eli answered with a touchdown pass of his own—a 34-yarder to **wide receiver** Plaxico Burress that cut the lead to 13-7 with just 32 seconds remaining in the first half. However, the Colts quickly struck back, as Vinatieri kicked a 48-yard field goal as time expired in the first half. As the two teams headed into the locker room, it was beginning to look like the Colts had taken charge of the game.

The Giants, though, were up for the challenge. Eli showed the type of moxie his older brother often displayed, as he led the Giants on an 11-play, 69-yard drive that was capped by a 15-yard touchdown pass to tight end Jeremy Shockey. But just as the Giants were gaining momentum, Eli **fumbled** the ball and the Colts recovered. Peyton then drove his team 51 yards on eight plays and running back Dominic Rhodes finished the drive with a one-yard touchdown run that put the Colts up 23-14 with 13:21 left in the game.

Little brother came right back, however, driving the Giants 78 yards in 11 plays, as running back Brandon Jacobs powered in from one yard out. The Giants had cut the lead to two points,

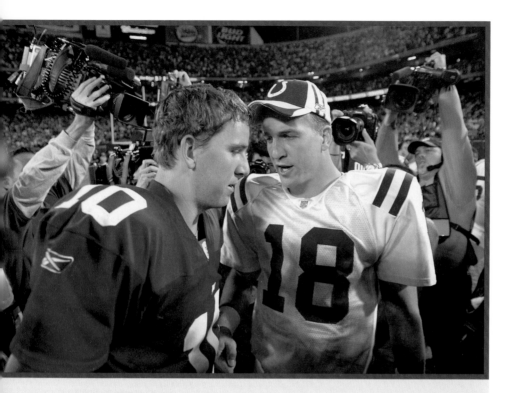

Peyton (right) and Eli Manning greet each other after the Indianapolis Colts' 26-21 win over the New York Giants on September 10, 2006. In the first meeting between the Manning brothers, Peyton completed 25 of 41 passes for 276 yards, one touchdown, and an interception; while Eli completed 20 of 34 passes for 247 yards, two touchdowns, and an interception.

with eight minutes remaining in the game. But that was the closest the Giants would get, as the Colts capped the scoring with yet another Vinatieri field goal with 2:39 to play. Eli and the Giants mounted one last drive, but they ran out of time, leaving the Colts the winners, 26-21.

The two brothers posted similar statistics. Peyton completed 25 of 41 passes for 276 yards. He had one touchdown and one **interception**. Eli completed 20 of 34 passes for 247 yards. He had two touchdowns and one interception. The *New*

*York Times* expressed it thus: "Colts Defeat Giants in Opener, but Battle of Mannings is a Tie."

Immediately after the game, Peyton headed straight for Eli. Hugging and patting his little brother on the head, Peyton expressed the love of an older brother for his younger brother. Surely, this would only be the first of several meetings between the brothers.

So what kind of family could produce two great NFL players? What is amazing is that it very well could have been *three*. Good genes is part of the answer, of course, but so is the social environment in which the Manning boys grew up. To understand them, and the contributions they have made to the NFL, one has to look no further than their father.

# Archie Who?

In the October 13, 1969, issue of *Sports Illustrated*, author Pat Putnam wrote a cover story titled "The SEC Catches On," detailing how the days of grind-it-out-on-the-ground football and the stout defenses of the storied Southeastern Conference had become passé, only to be replaced by quick-striking offenses. He wrote:

> Remember the South, the magnolias and mockingbirds and muddy roads, and the cane poles, and odor of wood smoke and somewhere, far off, the baying of hound dogs, and those big-iron-eyed Southeastern Conference football players who kicked the hawg out of a ball on third down and just dared someone to try and score? Ah, those great ante-bedlam days of the

7-3 scores, when any barefooted kid out of Opelousas or Pontonoc or Tuscumbia knew you could score five ways on defense. And that a six-point lead was better than a pond full of hungry catfish.

Putnam was lamenting the end of an era. The SEC, which had been known for knock-'em-down-drag-'em-out defensive struggles for two generations, had passed the torch to a new generation of offensive players, and scores such as 10-3 or 7-0 had become a thing of the past. He continued:

> Take, for instance, last week. Alabama and Ole Miss threw a combined 81 passes—and completed 55 of them, breaking an **NCAA** record—as Alabama won 33-32, which was just a little bitty score. LSU scored 63 points, all by itself. Tennessee scored 55. Mississippi State lost by 74. Just like that, snap! The stubborn old SEC is swinging, and the music isn't Grand Ole Opry.

College football had been big in the South since the 1920s, in part because there was little else to do on Saturday afternoons. Coaches such as Robert Neyland of Tennessee (pronounced Knee-land) and Paul "Bear" Bryant of Alabama took pride in their tough defenses. Southern teams were known for their ability to hold on to small leads for as long as a half and to keep the overall score under 20 points. Although it is hard to believe, during a 14-year stretch from 1926 to 1940, Neyland's Tennessee teams yielded only 485 points (which comes out to less than 35 points per season in a 9- or 10-game schedule)! The tradition of low scores and stout defenses continued until the late 1960s, when a new generation of college athletes, Archie Manning among them, lit up the SEC with new passing techniques that tripled or even quadrupled the number of points scored in a game.

University of Tennessee football coach Robert Neyland talks to team captain Ralph Hatley the day before the Volunteers squared off against Fordham University at the Polo Grounds on November 3, 1934. Neyland led Tennessee to four national titles and a record of 173–31–12 during his 21-year coaching career.

Archie Manning was born in Cleveland, Mississippi, in 1949, and grew up in Drew, in the northwestern part of that state. His father worked at a farm equipment store, and his mother—whom everyone called "Sis"—was a homemaker. The family reveled in many Southern traditions, including sports, the outdoors, and the virtues of country living.

Archie Manning (his full name was Elisha Archibald Manning) was an outstanding athlete at Drew High School, where he lettered in football, baseball, basketball, and track. Drew was, and is today, a small town, and opportunities for high school graduates were fairly limited at the time. Many a fine athlete hung up his cleats after high school to work in a dry goods store, for the railroad, or with the town highway crew, but Archie was so talented that he was able to leave Drew when he was offered a football scholarship to the University of Mississippi in Oxford, which is better known as "Ole Miss."

Oxford was the hometown of William Faulkner, one of America's most famous writers. Faulkner spent most of his life in Oxford, and his many books include characters from the surrounding landscape. Faulkner often criticized the South's history and traditions, but many students at Ole Miss simply took the Old South as it was—the land of magnolias, manners, and cotton fields. Archie Manning was one of those students; he later asserted that he loved the Old South and its traditions. But shortly after he entered Ole Miss, he started a new series of traditions, with his inspired play on the football field.

## ARCHIE AT OLE MISS

At six foot three (191 centimeters), 198 pounds (89.8 kilograms) and blessed with an unruly mane of red hair, Archie became extremely popular, whether on campus, in class, or on the football field. Ole Miss crowds loved to see Archie pass, but they became even more excited when he ran, for he was extremely elusive. In his three years at Ole Miss (he played on the freshman team his first season), Archie set many career records, including total offense (5,576 yards) and touchdown passes (56). Although both of these records have since been broken, he still holds an Ole Miss and SEC record that may never be eclipsed—total yards in a game. In a 33-32 loss to the University of Alabama on October 4, 1969, Archie passed for 436 yards and ran for another 104 for a total of 540 yards.

While Archie was at Ole Miss, the Rebels had many rivals, including Alabama. But in the late 1960s, the team's fiercest competition was with the University of Tennessee, whose nickname, the "Volunteers," came from the large number of Tennessee residents who volunteered to fight in the War of 1812 and the Mexican War. The annual contest between the Ole Miss Rebels and Tennessee Volunteers was one of the hottest events in town: Fans often purchased their tickets as much as a year in advance.

In the autumn of 1969, as Archie Manning was blazing a new path, with his inspired running and daring passing, an All-American **linebacker** at Tennessee was asked about Archie and the Ole Miss Rebels. When someone compared the Rebel players to horses, Steve Kiner scornfully replied in a *Sports Illustrated* article, "Hee-haw, them's not horses, them's mules." When asked about the tremendous athletic skill of Archie Manning, Kiner replied, "Archie who?"

That insult by Kiner was enough to prompt the writing of a song that became popular on the Ole Miss campus. Entitled "The Ballad of Archie Who," the Ole Miss football anthem was written by a postal clerk from Magnolia, Mississippi, and sung by a group called the Rebel Rousers. The recording sold an astounding 35,000 copies and let the Tennessee Volunteers know that Archie Manning was ready to lead Ole Miss to victory:

> The ball is on the fifty,
> The down is third and ten,
> He runs it down the sidelines;
> Yes, Archie takes it in.

The Rebels and Volunteers met in Jackson, Tennessee, on November 15, 1969. The game would go down as one of the biggest wins in the history of Ole Miss football. Ole Miss entered the game ranked eighteenth in the country, while Tennessee was ranked third. Archie wasted little time getting the Rebels on the scoreboard, as he led Ole Miss on an 11-play,

82-yard drive to take a 7-0 lead. He finished the drive by running the ball in from three yards out for a touchdown. Archie's coach, John Vaught, had told him to start with the running game, tire Tennessee out, and then take it to the air. It turned out to be unnecessary because Tennessee proved unable to stop the Ole Miss ground game.

The Rebels moved the ball 38 yards on their second drive, which ended in another touchdown. The third touchdown came soon after, and, as they say, the rout was on. When all was said and done, Ole Miss thrashed Tennessee, 38-0, with Archie leading the way. He completed 9 of 18 passes for 159 yards and one touchdown and ran for another. How was that for "Archie who?"

## A FAMILY TRAGEDY

In the summer before he led Ole Miss to an 8–3 record and a berth in the Sugar Bowl, where they defeated third-ranked Arkansas, 27-22, Archie had to deal with an event that would change his life. In August 1969, at about the same time that Hurricane Camille was barreling down on the Gulf Coast, Archie's father, Buddy, took his own life. Returning from the wedding of a friend, Archie found his father lying on his bed, having shot himself in the chest.

Making haste to clean things up so his mother and sister would not have to see the body, Archie quickly planned his future. Up to that moment, he had been a rather carefree young man, enjoying his time at Ole Miss and reveling in the praise he received from football fans. But his father's death changed everything, he believed, and soon after telling his mother the terrible news, Archie informed her that he would drop out of Ole Miss to become the man of the family; that he would provide for his mother and sister.

Not a chance, she replied. He had a promising career ahead of him, and she was not going to let him throw it away. She and

During his career at Ole Miss, Archie Manning threw for 4,753 yards and 56 touchdowns and ran for 823 yards. The two-time first-team All-SEC and All-American performer is pictured here leading Ole Miss to a 38-0 victory over Tennessee on November 15, 1969.

her daughter would care for themselves, and, somehow, they would find a way to make do. That was that.

Returning to Ole Miss, Archie continued his winning ways. Not only did he help the Rebels go 22–10–1 during his three years as the starting quarterback, but he became one of the most beloved students on campus. Friendly and unassuming, he was admired and loved, and his fame continued to grow. During his freshman year, Archie began dating the woman who would later become homecoming queen and his wife.

Olivia Williams did not take to Archie at first. She came from Philadelphia, Mississippi, a larger town than Drew. Archie had led his high school basketball team to an upset win against her high school team in the regional tournament. She disliked the brash youngster with the fiery red hair and thought he came across as a braggart and show-off. However, when they were formally introduced at Ole Miss, Olivia quickly warmed up to Archie, who she discovered was far from cocky. Everything seemed to fit: He would become the big man on campus; she was an engaging beauty; and she had a strong interest in sports. Before long she was attending all of Archie's football games and became one of his biggest fans. So began a three-year courtship that would lead to marriage in January 1971. Their future seemed bright indeed.

## THE NFL DRAFT AND NEW ORLEANS

Certain years of the NFL draft seem to include better players than others. Many football coaches labeled 1971 the "year of the quarterback," because Archie Manning of Ole Miss, Dan Pastorini of Santa Clara University, and Jim Plunkett of Stanford were all available that spring. Archie knew the benefits of being a top draft pick, but he also was aware of the pitfalls. In an attempt to bring parity to the 26 NFL teams, the league commissioner, Pete Rozelle, had decreed that the team with the worst record the year before (the worst win-loss ratio) would receive the first draft pick. The Boston Patriots finished 2–12, edging out the 2–11–1 Saints to claim the top draft pick. The Patriots selected Plunkett with the first pick, and the Saints took Manning with the second pick.

The Saints were a recent expansion team, having entered the **National Football Conference (NFC)** in 1967. They had struggled during their first few seasons, and the year that preceded Archie's arrival was their worst yet. In addition to their terrible record, the Saints scored a league-low 172 points, while yielding 347 to their opponents. The Saints were pinning their hopes on Archie to help turn the franchise around.

After they graduated from Ole Miss that spring, Archie and Olivia moved to New Orleans. The Crescent City, as it is called, had a population of approximately 700,000 at the time and was about equally divided between whites and African Americans. The Mannings settled in Metairie, a suburb of New Orleans,

## THE NFL IN 1971

Professional football was far from being a new sport in 1971, but it was not yet the all-consuming passion it is today. Football was growing in popularity, but baseball was still regarded by many as America's sport, and the traditional powers of today—such as the Pittsburgh Steelers, Dallas Cowboys, and New England Patriots—had not yet acquired their mystique.

The NFL was founded in 1920, but in 1960 it was challenged by a new league—the AFL (American Football League). The two leagues had played separate schedules for six years before football leaders engineered a merger in 1966, which would go into effect in 1970. The AFL became part of the NFL, and the identity of one, full-time professional football league was born. Still, the fame and glory that professional players receive today was not the same in 1971, the year Archie Manning was drafted by the Saints.

Many Manning fans lament the fact that Archie was drafted to play for the Saints, a newly formed expansion team. What if he had gone to the Pittsburgh Steelers, who were about to where they felt very much like country kids being introduced to life in the big city. Years later, Archie recalled in *The New Orleans Saints: 25 Years of Heroic Effort*:

> I think that when I first came there was a lot of pressure on me, although I'm not sure that I realized it at the time. I was kind of in a blaze of glory, I guess, from all the things that had happened at Ole Miss, all the notoriety there. And I guess it was magnified here somewhat, in that we'd played big games against LSU.

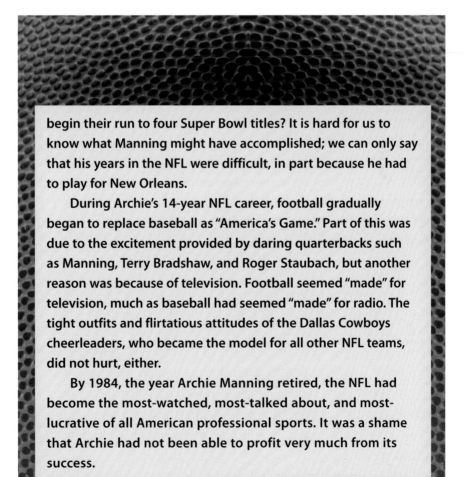

begin their run to four Super Bowl titles? It is hard for us to know what Manning might have accomplished; we can only say that his years in the NFL were difficult, in part because he had to play for New Orleans.

During Archie's 14-year NFL career, football gradually began to replace baseball as "America's Game." Part of this was due to the excitement provided by daring quarterbacks such as Manning, Terry Bradshaw, and Roger Staubach, but another reason was because of television. Football seemed "made" for television, much as baseball had seemed "made" for radio. The tight outfits and flirtatious attitudes of the Dallas Cowboys cheerleaders, who became the model for all other NFL teams, did not hurt, either.

By 1984, the year Archie Manning retired, the NFL had become the most-watched, most-talked about, and most-lucrative of all American professional sports. It was a shame that Archie had not been able to profit very much from its success.

Selected by New Orleans with the second overall pick in the 1971 NFL draft, Archie Manning spent much of his career being sacked or knocked down by opposing defenses. Here, Los Angeles Rams defensive end Fred Dryer sacks Manning during a 24-0 loss at the Los Angeles Coliseum on September 22, 1974.

Archie started off in magnificent fashion, leading the Saints to a very surprising 24-20 victory over the Los Angeles Rams. He completed 16 of 29 passes for 218 yards and a touchdown, while running for another, in one of the best NFL rookie quarterback performances to date. But the season itself was only a small improvement over the previous one: The Saints went 4–8–2 in 1971. They yielded exactly the same number of points as in 1970 (347), but they improved their offensive output to 266 points.

Few football players can escape injury, but Archie had his fair share during his college years (at one point he had broken both arms and one leg!). Things did not change much when he reached the NFL. The Saints' offensive line was not very good, and Archie was repeatedly knocked down and **sacked**. He showed plenty of resilience and determination, but the lone highlight for the Saints after their opening-day win against the Rams was their 24-14 victory against the defending Super Bowl champion Dallas Cowboys.

The following year was even worse for the Saints; they took a step back with a 2–11–1 record and scored only 215 points. In 1973, the team improved to 5–9, a record they repeated in 1974, but 1975 represented the nadir of their fortunes, with the team falling to 2–12, in a year when they scored only 165 points.

Yet in the midst of difficulty, and sometimes outright failure, Archie and Olivia Manning remained decidedly upbeat. The Saints *had* to get better, they reasoned; surely the team would pull out of the doldrums at some point. Off the field, life was a bit more rewarding: The Mannings had started a family. Their first son, Cooper, who was named for his maternal grandfather, was born in 1974, and a second son, Peyton, named for his father's uncle, followed two years later on March 24, 1976.

# Sons on the Rise

**B**oth Manning children were big—very big. Cooper and Peyton both weighed more than 11 pounds (5 kilograms) when they were born. Some people said the blessing was in their genes—a combination of their father's size and their mother's grace—but even that did not account for the fact that they would grow to be well over six feet tall.

The two seasons that followed Peyton's birth were not good ones for Archie. In 1976, the Saints hired Hank Stram, who led the Kansas City Chiefs to a victory in Super Bowl IV, as their fifth head coach in the franchise's short history. However, Stram and an injury-plagued Archie could do little to improve the Saints' fortunes, as the team went 4–10 in 1976 and 3–11 in 1977. Stram was fired after the 1977 season and replaced by Dick Nolan, who preferred to have his quarterback throw the ball more. Archie benefited from Nolan's new offense, posting the best three-year stretch of his career. In 1978, Archie led the Saints to a 7–9 record and completed 291 of 471 passes for 3,416 yards and 17 touchdowns on his way to being named NFC MVP. In 1979, the Saints finally made it to the .500 mark, at 8–8, but just when it appeared they were ready to take the next step and perhaps challenge for a playoff berth, they bottomed out. The Saints went 1–15 in 1980, a season in which they yielded 487 points while scoring only 291. The Saints were last, dead last, in almost every NFL statistical category.

No one was more disappointed than Archie, who had enjoyed such great success in college. In New Orleans, he was tethered to the worst team in the league, one whose fans showed their embarrassment by wearing paper bags over their heads. However, through it all, Archie did not complain. New Orleans fans came to adore Archie in a new way, not for his tremendous skill, but for his greatness as a human being. Try as they might, newspaper reporters could not persuade Archie to criticize his team or his teammates. People began to call him "Saint Archie."

## THE MANNING FAMILY

Young Peyton and Cooper knew little of their father's travails on the football field, because Archie was invariably cheerful and interested in them when he came home each night. Even after a hard game and a tough loss, he was a devoted father, playing with them, letting them massage his stiff limbs, and so forth. After all, Archie's father had taken his life and never told his son that he loved him. Archie promised himself that he would have a different relationship with his children. Despite the tranquility at home, sometimes the boys were exposed to the frustrations of Saints fans when they attended the team's games in the Louisiana Superdome, which opened in 1975.

On one occasion, during the putrid 1980 season, Olivia and her two sons were watching Archie play a dreadful game

Archie Manning takes a knee on the sideline during a game at the Louisiana Superdome in the 1970s. During his 10 seasons with New Orleans, the Saints were just 41–104–3, causing Manning to spend a good deal of time in contemplation.

against the Los Angeles Rams. The fans at the Superdome started to boo, and Cooper and Peyton asked if they could boo, too. Without waiting for an answer, they started to sound off. Embarrassed and furious, Olivia left the boys at home for the next few games.

Peyton and Cooper were natural rivals from day one; they competed with each other in all kinds of sports, including pickup games of every category. The two brothers were pleased at the arrival of a third brother, Eli, who was born in 1981. Pictures from this time period show a serene Olivia Manning holding one rather chubby baby (much like his older brothers), while Cooper and Peyton frolicked on the carpet or did headstands for the camera. Just as life was truly coming together for the Manning family, Archie's professional career began to fall apart.

Archie had always done his best for the New Orleans Saints, but there was a limit to what one player could do for a team. After the terrible 1980 season, which seemed to define the Saints, Archie played in only 12 games during the 1981 season and then was traded to the Houston Oilers just 10 days into the start of the 1982 season. For someone who had been so loyal to the Saints, the trade must have hurt, but Archie welcomed the chance for a new start.

Unfortunately, Houston proved little better than New Orleans. Archie played in just six games for the Oilers in 1982, but he did have the good fortune of being able to visit his family whenever he wanted. The flight time between Houston and New Orleans was relatively short, so Archie often flew home after practice sessions to be with his family. Although he was only in his early 30s, Archie knew his days as an NFL player were coming to an end. He certainly had not made the kind of splash he thought he could have made, but he had a happy family and had made more money during his career than he could have imagined when he was growing up in Drew. Life was good, even though his football career was not.

The Houston Oilers traded Archie in 1983. He was sent north, to chilly Minneapolis, to play for the Minnesota Vikings. The Vikings were actually an improvement, in that they had traditionally been a winning team, having reached four Super Bowls since 1969 (though they had lost all four). The whole Manning family went north to Minnesota in the fall of 1983, but they did not stay long. Olivia and the children disliked the cold weather, and Archie was forced to stick it out through a long season after his family went home. A year later, Vikings head coach Les Steckel suggested it was time for Archie to think about retirement. Although he had long resisted the idea in his mind, Archie jumped at the chance, especially after the Vikings lost a franchise-record 13 games in 1984. He was still young, relatively healthy, and he had more money than he thought possible. This was the right moment, he decided. He later explained the decision in the book *Manning*:

> Never look back, Never. And I haven't. When I finally left the Vikings, it was an upper instead of a downer, a plus instead of a minus. Good-bye football, hello rest of my life. And hello Cooper, Peyton, and Eli, and the football I would enjoy through them. A whole new world.

Two seasons in Minnesota were enough for Archie, and in 1984, he hung up his cleats for good. He had children to raise and educate.

One thing Archie did not admit to himself at the time he retired was how distanced he felt from his youngest son. Five years younger than Peyton and seven years younger than Cooper, Eli had not grown up to see his father play in New Orleans. Worse, Archie's short stints in Houston and Minnesota took him so far away that young Eli sometimes ignored Archie when he returned home. Knowing how important family is, Archie recommitted himself to being an exemplary father and to developing a new trust and association with Eli. Meanwhile, the two older boys were in elementary school and were beginning to grow up.

By now the Mannings had settled into their dream home in New Orleans' Garden District. Archie and Olivia wanted the very best for their children, so it was a given the boys would apply to Isidore Newman High School, a prestigious, academically oriented private school in uptown New Orleans. Although it boasted fine academic programs and many impressive graduates (see sidebar on pages 30–31), Newman also had a variety of sports programs, ranging from gymnastics to football. Despite its small size, Newman has won several state championships in Class 1A and 2A.

By the time they attended Newman, Cooper and Peyton were both big and gangly for their age. Inheriting size and strength from both sides of the family, they were on their way to becoming six foot four (193 centimeters) and six foot five (196 centimeters), respectively, but this did not automatically make them stars on the Newman teams. Peyton, especially, was concerned with his slow foot speed, which got worse after a bout with tendonitis. Cooper, gifted with all sorts of athletic ability, was so carefree (he was the family jokester) that people wondered if he would live up to his athletic potential. Here is what their father thought of them at the time, as recounted in the book *Manning*:

> Actually, I saw Cooper's ability first. Not just because he was older, but of the two he was the better athlete growing up. Or at least the more versatile. . . . Peyton, on the other hand, was a natural *quarterback*. Built that way, thought that way, and always willing to outwork everybody else to make it happen.

Peyton and Cooper had both grown up in the shadow of their father's legend and were well aware of his legacy. They knew how wonderful a professional football career could be, but they also knew there were drawbacks. However, they were not particularly concerned about the drawbacks, because by the time Cooper was a senior and Peyton a sophomore, at Newman High School, they were sure they wanted to play in the NFL. Archie Manning discouraged them from getting ahead of themselves; he told the boys to concentrate on the here and now, to enjoy the high school games they were currently playing. They certainly did.

Football was big in the Manning home, but it was not everything—not by a long shot. Not only did Archie and Olivia encourage their children to become involved in community service, but they also went to church on a regular basis. One day, while he was in his teens, Peyton had a life-changing experience while he was at church. From that day on, faith came first in his life, family came second, and football came third. He did not often speak about his faith; like many truly religious people, he carried his faith quietly, but not lightly.

## THE GLORIOUS SEASON

The autumn of 1991 proved to be the moment when Cooper and Peyton began to display their talents on the football field. Starting as quarterback in his sophomore year, Peyton threw pass after pass to his older brother, who was a star wide receiver.

## ISIDORE NEWMAN

Visitors to schools and colleges often enter halls, dorms, and buildings named for notable people, yet the identities of those individuals often go unrecognized. This is not the case with Isidore Newman, a person who left a lasting mark on New Orleans and the high school he founded.

Born in Bavaria (in southern Germany) in 1837, Newman came to the United States in 1853 as a penniless 16-year-old. Fortunately, he had family in New Orleans, and he worked with his cousins in a money-changing business that catered to sailors who had just arrived in New Orleans. Thanks to his good business acumen, Newman rose to establish his own banking and brokerage firm and was a noted philanthropist. He became the owner of nearly all of the (now) famous streetcar lines in New Orleans and was among the first to make the lines electric. In 1903, at the age of 66, he endowed the Isidore Newman Manual Training School. The first priority was to educate children from the Jewish

"Manning to Manning" was the expression heard around New Orleans that fall, as the brothers led Newman all the way to the Louisiana Class 2A state semifinals before losing to Haynesville, 27-21. In typical family fashion, Cooper took the loss in stride—almost with ease—while Peyton agonized over the missed opportunities. He was already becoming one of the fiercest devotees of watching game film of other teams and was known as the teammate who spent the most time in the weight room. Cooper, on the other hand, was the free spirit who delighted in all sorts of pranks. The two brothers seemed to

Orphans' Home on nearby St. Charles Avenue; the second was to educate any other children who lived in the neighborhood and wanted to attend the school. When Newman died in 1909, he provided for 28 different charities—a fine legacy for a man who, earlier in life, had been derided by the *New Orleans Times Democrat* as a selfish man, uninterested in the welfare of the public.

Renamed the Isidore Newman School in 1931, the private high school has many distinguished alumni in various fields, including sports, writing, leadership, and the arts. Painter and naturalist Walter Inglis Anderson was an early graduate; Rhodes Scholar and former *Time* magazine managing editor Walter Isaacson graduated in 1970; and Michael Lewis, who graduated in 1979, is the author of *The Blind Side: Evolution of a Game*, about professional football. All three Manning children graduated from Newman, as did Christopher Rice, a best-selling author and the son of New Orleans novelist Anne Rice.

Cooper Manning (left) and his younger brother Peyton talk during football practice at Isidore Newman High School in 1991. Cooper was an all-state wide receiver at Newman before his football career was cut short by spinal stenosis, a narrowing of the spinal canal that can lead to paralysis.

have inherited different aspects of their parents' personalities: Olivia Manning had always been more easygoing, while Archie had been the taskmaster, though never a pushy parent when it came to sports. (He insisted on the boys *playing* sports rather than thinking about professional futures.)

In the fall of 1991, it was a foregone conclusion that Cooper would go to Ole Miss, the alma mater of both Archie and Olivia. Peyton hoped to go there as well, and the brothers intended to pick up where the dynamic duo had left off: using a razzle-dazzle combination of Manning to Manning to lead the Rebels to victories on the gridiron. But these plans were not to come to fruition.

During the latter part of the football season and during the beginning of the basketball season at Newman, Cooper started experiencing numbness in his fingers, and at other times he lost strength in his hands. He lost weight as well, leading Archie to take him to a number of doctors after the basketball season ended. The problem was misdiagnosed, which led Cooper to have surgery on his ulnar nerve that summer. Cooper made it to Ole Miss that fall, where he began to participate in fall football practice. But when he began to complain of pain once again, the team doctor urged him to get a second opinion. Finally, a doctor at Texas's Baylor Medical Center gave him the crushing news that he had spinal stenosis, a narrowing of the spinal canal that makes paralysis a distinct possibility. In fact, doctors told the family it was almost a miracle that Cooper had not suffered a life-changing injury while playing at Newman his senior season.

Football, for Cooper, was over.

At the time, Cooper sent a letter to Peyton that conveyed his sentiments during the difficult time. The letter was reprinted in Jimmy Hyams's book, *Peyton Manning: Primed and Ready*:

I would like to live my dream of playing football through you. Although I cannot play anymore, I know

I can still get the same feeling out of watching my little brother do what he does best. I know now that we are good for each other, because I need you to be serious and look at things from a different perspective. I am good for you, as well, to take things light. I love you, Peyt, and only great things lay ahead for you. Thanks for everything on and off the field.

Peyton had always been a serious child, and some people would later claim he was born serious. But his brother's life-threatening condition, and the knowledge that, at any time, his football career could also come to a sudden end, made a distinct impression. Peyton would, in some ways, carry the torch for his older brother, as well as for his beloved father, on the football field.

# Ole Rocky Top

During his junior and senior seasons at Newman, Peyton Manning returned to the football field with something to prove. Perhaps he felt obligated to Cooper, who could no longer play football, or perhaps he wanted to silence critics of his father—those who said Archie had not done all he could while playing for the New Orleans Saints. In either case, Manning was determined to succeed on the football field.

## SENIOR YEAR

In the fall of 1993, Manning was one of the most heavily recruited football players in the country. The college coaches who came to watch him play used superlatives such as "the best," or "the most talented all-around player," to describe Manning. A major recruiting battle soon began, with more than 60 colleges trying to convince the 17-year-old to commit to their school. Following his senior season, Manning was named the Gatorade National Player of the Year after passing for 2,703 yards and 39 touchdowns. During his three years as Newman's starting quarterback, Manning led the team to a 34–5 record.

Manning stayed remarkably levelheaded throughout the process, which he viewed as a business venture. His father had studied business at Ole Miss, and Manning had thoughts of doing the same in college, but at which school? In the end, it came to down to a list of four:

- Notre Dame, because of its great tradition of passing quarterbacks
- Ole Miss, largely for sentimental reasons
- The University of Tennessee, because the Volunteers had a new coach and were passing the ball more
- The University of Florida, because the Gators also passed the ball a lot

Of this list of schools, Ole Miss was the weakest contender. Manning certainly considered his father's and mother's alma mater, but, although Ole Miss had won nine games in two out of the last four seasons, it did not have the tradition of Notre Dame or Tennessee. Naturally, Manning had some trepidation about considering Tennessee, which had been his father's chief rival during his playing days. All-American linebacker Steve Kiner had disrespected Ole Miss with his "Archie who?" question back in 1969. But the more Manning thought about it, the more he had to conclude that Tennessee was on the verge of becoming—if it was not already—the best team in the Southeastern Conference. In 1993, the Tennessee Volunteers finished eleventh in the nation at 10–2 and led the NCAA in several offensive categories, including highest average yards gained per rush (5.9 yards), per play (6.9 yards), and points per game (an astounding 42.8). Tennessee scored 62 touchdowns

During the 1992 season, Phillip Fulmer took over as Tennessee head coach after Johnny Majors suffered a heart attack. Fulmer led the Volunteers to a 10–2 record in 1993 and was able to persuade Peyton Manning to attend Tennessee thanks in large part to the Volunteers' pass-friendly offense.

that year, the most in the nation, and had the highest number of points scored directly after **kickoff**. In addition, Manning felt more comfortable with the Tennessee coaches. "Coach Fulmer and the other coaches did a good job just being my friends," he told *Sporting News*. "They didn't sell the school too much. They just wanted to be friends. In the end, I felt comfortable spending four years with them."

The long recruiting process came down to a press conference in New Orleans, held on January 25, 1994. Manning remained calm throughout the press conference, explaining that he had opted to attend the University of Tennessee and wear the orange and white rather than the red, white, and blue of Ole Miss. Perhaps he thought his decision would be the last word, but the controversy had just begun.

Thousands of Ole Miss fans were dismayed and angry that Archie Manning's star quarterback son had chosen to play for the enemy. Manning received a lot of hate mail, with letters that suggested he break a leg in practice, and worse, but his father

## THE GENERAL AND HIS STADIUM

Some coaches are forever identified with a team, a college, or a set of colors. Such is the case with Paul "Bear" Bryant of Alabama, Vince Lombardi of the Green Bay Packers, and Johnny Unitas of the Baltimore Colts. But few coaches have been so thoroughly identified with a school and a winning tradition as Robert Neyland and the University of Tennessee.

Born in Texas in 1892, Neyland was a star football player (he also boxed and played baseball) at the U.S. Military Academy at West Point, where he graduated in 1916. After serving in France during World War I, he arrived at the University of Tennessee in 1926 and became professor of military science and the head football coach. After coaching back-to-back undefeated teams in 1938 and 1939, he returned to the U.S. Army and rose to the rank of brigadier general during World War II before retiring from the army in 1946. During his time at Tennessee, Neyland became one of the most successful coaches in college football history. Disdaining heroics and inspired speeches, he focused on fundamentals, especially on the defensive side of the ball.

took the brunt of the criticism. Archie Manning, the letters declared, should have insisted his son go to Ole Miss. Some letters even suggested that Archie should remain in New Orleans and not come to Mississippi any time soon.

Archie was saddened by the letters, but he was also, privately, appalled. What had happened to the state of the world when so-called "fans" threatened to harm someone because he chose to attend a certain school? Archie and Olivia would have loved to see Peyton go to Ole Miss—to

To this day, his 1939 team holds the all-time NCAA record for consecutive quarters (71) in which opponents did not score.

At the end of World War II, Neyland returned to Tennessee to find the rules, and styles of the game, had changed. However, he refused to shift from the single-wing **formation** to the "T" formation and continued to have great success as a coach. During his 21-year career, his teams went 173–31–12 and won four national titles. Neyland retired after the 1952 season, but his spirit lived on, both in the Tennessee style of play and in the new Neyland Stadium, which was renamed in his honor in 1961.

Neyland Stadium is the third-largest on-campus college football stadium in the country, and one of only two that can be approached by water (the University of Washington's Husky Stadium is the other). The enormous stadium can hold more than 102,000 spectators, which it often did during Peyton Manning's four-year career.

continue the grand family tradition there—but they had left the decision up to him. Now it was their time to defend him, as well as themselves, from the verbal assaults. As Peyton recounted in *Manning*:

> Dad started getting calls right away. Indignant calls, outraged calls, what's-going-on calls. *Brutal* calls. We both got blasted hard by Ole Miss people, and while it hurt me a lot, it hurt mainly because of what it did to my dad. He was devastated. . . . He *didn't* deserve this.

There was little Archie and Olivia could do, but Cooper Manning, then in his sophomore year at Ole Miss, could do a lot. He began wearing Tennessee colors and spoke about the virtues of the Tennessee athletic program. But all the talk, and back talk, came to nothing. Peyton enrolled at the University of Tennessee in the autumn of 1994.

## A NEW BEGINNING IN KNOXVILLE

Manning arrived at Tennessee in July to learn that he was one of four potential quarterbacks who would be fighting for the starting **position**. He and fellow freshman Branndon Stewart were the **backups** to veterans Jerry Colquitt and Todd Helton. Given that many observers ranked Manning and Stewart about equal in talent, and that both of them had no experience, it seemed a long shot as to whether Manning would even see any action in 1994. He professed not to care, saying it was fine to be "redshirted" (to sit out and retain four years of eligibility) for his freshman year, but people who knew Manning doubted he could be so calm about the matter. Then destiny called.

In the very first game, at UCLA, Manning benefited from an unfortunate set of circumstances. Starting quarterback Jerry Colquitt blew out his knee in the first half and Manning was surprisingly summoned to play, rather than Helton. Manning

In the first game of Peyton Manning's freshman season against fourteenth-ranked UCLA, he was thrust into action after Tennessee's starting quarterback was knocked out of the game. Although the thirteenth-ranked Volunteers lost to the Bruins that day, Manning got valuable experience in a hostile environment and would go on to become a four-year starter at Tennessee.

hastened to the field, where he tried to assure the older, more seasoned, players in the **huddle**. He knew he was just a freshman, Manning said to them, but he could and would lead them down the field.

The players quickly responded, "Shut up and call the [expletive deleted] play!" Manning recalled in *Peyton Manning: Primed and Ready.*

A bit shocked, Manning played just that series. Helton ended up rallying the team, but Tennessee lost the game, 25-23. Despite the setback, Manning had his first test under fire. In the next game against Georgia, Manning did not play, but he saw some action the following week against Florida.

## TAKING OVER

In the fourth game of the season, against Mississippi State, backup quarterback Todd Helton also suffered a season-ending knee injury. With both veteran quarterbacks now out for the year, Manning and fellow freshman Branndon Stewart would compete for the starting job. There were plenty of accusations on both sides, with Stewart's mother claiming that Peyton was given all the breaks because his father was Archie Manning, and some humorous incidents as when she banged on a locker room door, demanding to be admitted because she was sure Archie was inside. But slowly and surely, Manning won the starting position.

Was he more talented? Perhaps.

Did he throw the ball better? Probably.

The main reason, however, was that Manning was willing to work as hard as possible to win the starting position. From his earliest years, he had been a competitor, fighting his older brother, Cooper (who usually had the upper hand), and now he saw a golden opportunity to become the starting quarterback. By the middle of the 1994 season, Manning had become the man, and he never relinquished the starting spot during his time at Tennessee.

Despite his hard work, Manning and the Volunteers had an average year by Tennessee standards. They lost to UCLA, beat Georgia, and then got shellacked by archrival Florida, 31-0.

## THE SOUTHEASTERN CONFERENCE

Those who know college football claim the Southeastern Conference (SEC) is the most competitive conference in the country. Founded in 1932, the SEC started with 13 teams but today has 12. From the very beginning, the SEC attracted a stronger fan base than was true with many northern and western conferences; the reason, it is believed, was that there was less to do on Saturdays in the Old South. Fans began to develop a powerful love of their teams and a deep hatred for their opponents.

Over the decades, 'Bama (that is, the University of Alabama) won more SEC championships than any other school (21). This was largely due to the inspired coaching of Paul "Bear" Bryant. But Tennessee is not far behind (13), and Ole Miss has even won six conference titles over the years. During the last two decades, the University of Florida has become a powerhouse and has won seven titles since 1991. Former head coach Steve Spurrier brought an intense (some said diabolical) approach to the game. Florida fans responded by making Ben Hill Griffin Stadium, aka, "The Swamp," the most difficult place to play for opposing teams.

Despite Florida's recent upswing, six different schools have won SEC titles during the last 10 seasons, which makes the conference ultracompetitive. Unfortunately for Tennessee fans, the Volunteers' last SEC title came in 1998, when they also won their last national title, defeating Florida State, 23-16, in the Fiesta Bowl to cap an undefeated 13-0 season.

The Volunteers struggled a bit after that, but came on strong toward the end, defeating Kentucky, 52-0, and Vanderbilt, 65-0. Tennessee was invited to the Gator Bowl, where it beat Virginia Tech, 45-23, to finish 8–4. In just one season, Manning had accomplished what he had set out to do, but would he be able to retain the starting role in 1995?

After a relaxing 1995 summer, Manning was back for his sophomore season. A serious student, he majored in speech communication and minored in business, earning high marks from the start. But he was also a serious devotee of the game of football, spending hours studying film of his SEC rivals. Although Manning was too smart to comment openly, he probably recognized that he was the most polished quarterback in the SEC, but that did not mean he and Tennessee would win the SEC title. There was much more that went into winning a title.

The Volunteers started off well, beating East Carolina and Georgia, but they were easily defeated by Florida, 62-37. Tennessee recovered and went on to defeat Mississippi State, Oklahoma State, and eighteenth-ranked Arkansas, but sweetest of all was the 41-14 victory against twelfth-ranked Alabama in Birmingham. It was the first time the Volunteers had defeated the Crimson Tide since 1985, and it established Manning as a genuine folk hero in Knoxville. Just midway through his second season, he was "the man." He and the Volunteers went on to beat South Carolina, Southern Mississippi, Kentucky, and Vanderbilt for a 10–1 regular-season record, Tennessee's best since 1989, when they finished fifth in the country. But Florida won the SEC that year, and Manning had to be content with an appearance in the Citrus Bowl, where he and the Volunteers beat fourth-ranked Ohio State, 20-14, to finish number three in the country.

## JUNIOR YEAR

By the fall of 1996, Manning's celebrity status was continuing to grow. (By the time he graduated, he would even have

On September 9, 1995, Peyton Manning led eighth-ranked Tennessee to a 30-27 win over Georgia. Despite losing to fourth-ranked Florida the following week, the Volunteers finished the season 11–1 and ranked third in the nation.

a street near Neyland Stadium named after him.) Part of the reason Manning was so well loved was because he was quick to sign autographs (even when the demand was high) and because he did a lot of volunteer work in the Knoxville community. Speech communication was his major, and Manning showed his stuff on many an occasion. By his junior year, he had become nearly as beloved in Tennessee as his father had been at Ole Miss, all those years ago.

The 1996 season started off with a bang. The second-ranked Volunteers thrashed the University of Nevada–Las Vegas, 62-3, and took down UCLA, 35-20. But the effort and passion ran into the same brick wall. This time fourth-ranked Florida came north to play at Neyland Stadium, and though the game was much closer, the Gators still won, 35-29. Manning and the Volunteers went on to win the rest of their SEC games, beating Mississippi, Georgia, Alabama, South Carolina, Arkansas, Kentucky, and Vanderbilt, but they still finished second to Florida in the conference. Once again, Tennessee had to settle for the Citrus Bowl, where it beat eleventh-ranked Northwestern, 48-28, to cap a 10–2 season and a second straight top-10 finish. Now the stage was set for an emotional decision.

## COLLEGE OR THE PROS?

In January 1997, Manning stood at a crossroads. He was an academic All-American, with better than a 3.5 grade-point average, and he had compiled enough credits to graduate that June. His parents' desire for him to earn his college degree was assured. But Manning was getting plenty of calls from NFL scouts. Legally, they could not make any real overtures until he declared himself for the draft, but many draft experts projected him as a first-round pick, which could earn him in the neighborhood of $15 to $20 million.

Typically, Manning always weighed his options carefully. His father arranged for him to meet with a number of professional athletes, men who could help him make an informed decision. In January and February 1997, Manning met with former New York Giants quarterback Phil Simms, with former Dallas Cowboys quarterback Roger Staubach, and others. Plenty of advice was given—not all of it good.

In reality, Manning was in a different position than nearly all of these former NFL greats. With a college degree already in hand, and with the explosive talent he had shown on the college football field, he could truly write his own ticket. Some of the greats with whom he spoke (Roger Staubach, for example) had been in much weaker bargaining positions when they started in the NFL.

Manning announced his decision to the press on March 5, 1997. He would stay at Tennessee, and play another year, even though he could have entered the NFL draft and possibly been the number-one overall pick. When pressed to give his reasons, Manning explained that his father's best memories were of his college football days, and that he was not ready to give up his experience as a college student-athlete. Most who knew him credited Manning with having made the decision very much on his own. (Even Archie had suspected Peyton would go to the pros that year.)

## PEYTON MANNING'S STATISTICS AT TENNESSEE

| YEAR | ATT. | COMP. | PCT. | YDS. | TD | INT. |
|---|---|---|---|---|---|---|
| 1994 | 144 | 89 | 61.8 | 1,141 | 11 | 6 |
| 1995 | 380 | 244 | 64.2 | 2,954 | 22 | 4 |
| 1996 | 380 | 243 | 63.9 | 3,287 | 20 | 12 |
| 1997 | 477 | 287 | 60.2 | 3,819 | 36 | 11 |
| TOTALS | 1,381 | 863 | 62.5 | 11,201 | 89 | 33 |

As recounted in *Manning*, a reporter pressed Peyton on what had led him to his decision. What would he "get" this coming year that he had not had in the past three? Knowing that the reporter was looking for an angle, Manning replied, "A scholarship, room and board, and the right to call one play a game. I also get to drive Coach Fulmer's Lexus."

# The Big Time

By the autumn of 1997, Peyton Manning was recognized far and wide. Famed for his skill of throwing the football and admired for his work with charitable organizations, he was also lauded for having chosen to stay one more year in Knoxville. Coach Phillip Fulmer was perhaps the happiest of all; his star performer had come back for one more try at an SEC championship, and another attempt at dethroning the hated Florida Gators.

## LAST TRY

The Big Volunteers-Gators game was played on September 20, 1997, in Gainesville. Manning and the fourth-ranked Volunteers had a real chance in the game, but they never led, and the second-ranked Gators once again defeated the

Volunteers, 33-20. From there it was on to play Ole Miss in Knoxville. Manning's team (that was what many people started to call it) won the game rather easily, 31-17. Tennessee then beat thirteenth-ranked Georgia, 38-13; Alabama (making it twice in a row!), 38-21; South Carolina, 22-7; Southern Mississippi, 44-20; and Arkansas, 30-22. They closed out the regular season by beating Kentucky, 59-31, and squeaking past Vanderbilt, 17-10, which clinched a spot in their first SEC Championship Game. (After defeating Tennessee, Florida had lost to LSU and Georgia, which allowed the Volunteers to clinch the SEC East Division.) In the title game against eleventh-ranked Auburn, third-ranked Tennessee got by the Tigers, 30-29. With the win, Tennessee faced second-ranked Nebraska in the Orange Bowl. Unfortunately, the Cornhuskers easily defeated the Volunteers, 42-17, as Tennessee finished 11–2 and ranked seventh in the nation.

Manning passed for 3,819 yards and 36 touchdowns during his senior season and finished runner-up to Michigan **cornerback** Charles Woodson for the Heisman Trophy. During his Tennessee career, he set many school records, including career passing attempts (1,381), completions (863), passing yards (11,201), and touchdown passes (89). Despite Manning's many accomplishments, all the hoopla of four very exciting years

## HEISMAN TROPHY VOTING—1997

| | PLAYER | COLLEGE | CLASS | POSITION | VOTES |
|---|---|---|---|---|---|
| 1 | Charles Woodson | Michigan | Junior | Cornerback | 1,815 |
| 2 | Peyton Manning | Tennessee | Senior | Quarterback | 1,543 |
| 3 | Ryan Leaf | Washington State | Junior | Quarterback | 861 |
| 4 | Randy Moss | Marshall | Soph. | Wide Receiver | 253 |
| 5 | Ricky Williams | Texas | Junior | Running Back | 65 |

had come to an end and it was time to move on. Where would Manning go next? The NFL for certain, but which team?

## THE NFL DRAFT

The National Football League draft takes place every spring, at the end of April. During the years that have passed since Archie Manning was the number-two overall pick in the 1971 draft, much controversy has developed around the whole affair. Did it lead to better teams or better individual careers? Was the process too weighted in favor of the teams that had the worst record the preceding year?

Manning was aware of the controversy, and he probably harbored his own opinions on the matter, but it was not something he—or any other star player—could worry about. He had to sit through the process, waiting to be picked. That year, the first overall pick would come down to Manning or Washington State quarterback Ryan Leaf. The same age as Manning (they were born seven weeks apart), Leaf was a strong-armed quarterback who led the Cougars to the Pac-10 title and the school's first appearance in the Rose Bowl since 1931. Unfortunately for Leaf, there were disturbing rumors that he was undisciplined and a bit of a hothead, and this seemed to manifest itself on the opening day of the draft.

Standing six foot five (196 centimeters), Manning weighed in at a solid but sleek 230 pounds (104 kilograms). Standing perhaps an inch taller, Leaf came in at 261 pounds (118 kilograms), between 20 to 30 pounds (9 to 14 kilograms) over his target weight. How, people asked, could he be so cavalier about the draft process; not getting in shape for whomever was going to select him? Manning appeared quietly pleased that his big rival had misplayed his hand (or his weight), and the momentum of the draft soon turned to Manning. He was chosen as the number-one pick overall, going to the Indianapolis Colts, who had had a 2–14 record in 1997.

Peyton Manning was selected by the Indianapolis Colts with the number-one overall pick of the 1998 NFL draft. Manning is pictured here with Colts owner Jim Irsay (left) and NFL commissioner Paul Tagliabue (right) during the draft at New York City's Madison Square Garden.

(Under NFL draft rules, the team with the worst record during the prior season has first pick.)

### ROOKIE YEAR

Manning started his first NFL season on September 6, 1998, but he was not the only new face on the Colts' **sideline** that day. New head coach Jim Mora was making his debut with the Colts after 10 1/2 seasons with the New Orleans Saints. During his stint in New Orleans, Mora led the Saints to their first playoff appearance (and four overall) and their first NFC West Division title in franchise history. Now he was ready for a new challenge. Mora and his rookie quarterback faced the Miami Dolphins at home in their first game. To say this was an important game for Manning is an understatement, for he had long admired Dolphins quarterback Dan Marino (considered one of the all-time greats at that position). Manning had a pretty good debut, completing 21 of 37 passes for 302 yards, but he did throw three interceptions in the 24-15 loss. The following week, the Colts faced the New England Patriots on the road. Manning again threw three interceptions in a 29-6 loss that left the Colts with an 0–2 record.

Manning's competitiveness and steadfastness were already becoming known throughout the league, but, like almost every other rookie quarterback, he had a hard time adjusting to the NFL. The players were so much bigger (on average), faster, and more savvy than they were on the college level. Manning preferred to stay in the **pocket**, and he was not fleet of foot; nonetheless, he was astounded at how fast the players were on defense.

In Week 3, the Colts again hit the road, traveling to Giants Stadium to face the New York Jets. Again, Indianapolis had trouble scoring, as they were pounded by New York, 44-6. The embarrassing loss was the Colts' worst defeat that season and one of the most one-sided scores of the entire 1998 NFL season. There were some critics and commentators who felt the Colts should bench Manning, but the team had a lot invested in him, so that was not an option. They believed it was just a matter of time before Manning started to light up the scoreboard.

Manning justified some of their faith in him on September 27, when he completed 19 of 32 passes for 309 yards (his best total yet) against his father's old team, the New Orleans Saints. Despite the solid performance, Manning was intercepted three times and the Colts lost, 19-13, in overtime. The loss dropped the Colts to 0-4, and some fans and football experts wondered if young Peyton Manning was as good as he had been heralded just a few months earlier. Finally, on October 4, Manning and the Colts got their first win, defeating the San Diego Chargers (and Ryan Leaf), 17-12. Manning downplayed the importance of a Leaf-Manning rivalry, saying in *Manning,* "Neither Ryan nor I played very well. We won by playing less poorly." Manning was right: He completed just 12 of 23 passes for 137 yards and a touchdown, while Leaf only threw for 160 yards.

The following week, the Colts lost a close one to the Buffalo Bills, 31-24, and then had a thrilling matchup with San Francisco. The 49ers were not the team they had been during the 1980s and early 1990s, but they were still a playoff team and had Steve Young at quarterback. In the game, Young passed for 331 yards, and the 49ers won, 34-31. Despite the loss, the Colts played well, and for the first time that season, Manning did not throw an interception. Unfortunately, they dropped their next two games—to New England and Miami—to fall to 1–8 on the season. But on November 15, they got revenge against the Jets, clipping them, 24-23, as Manning completed 26 of 44 passes for 276 yards and three touchdowns.

Manning seldom revealed how he felt during his difficult rookie season, but he always confided in Archie and turned to him for advice. No one knew better than Archie how different the NFL was from college ball and the demands placed upon a rookie quarterback. There may have been times Manning questioned his ability, but he had to look no further than his father to be inspired. After all, things had to get better at some point.

As the season marched toward the end of November, the Colts lost to Buffalo, 34-11, and to the Baltimore Ravens, 38-31. However, in the loss to Baltimore, Manning had his best game of the season: He completed 27 of 42 passes for 357 yards and three touchdowns. By this time, observers were quite impressed with his arm strength and accuracy. Most rookies had a tough time "reading" defenses and knowing where to throw the ball, but Manning was coming on strong. He did

Peyton Manning drops back in the pocket during the Colts' 38-31 loss to the Baltimore Ravens on November 29, 1998. Despite the setback, Manning had the best game of his rookie season, completing 27 of 42 passes for 357 yards and three touchdowns.

## MOST PASSING YARDS DURING ROOKIE SEASON IN NFL HISTORY

| NUMBER | PLAYER |
|--------|--------|
| 3,739 | **Peyton Manning, Indianapolis Colts, 1998** |
| 2,931 | **Chris Weinke, Carolina Panthers, 2001** |
| 2,833 | **Rick Mirer, Seattle Seahawks, 1993** |

receive some negative comments from Baltimore Ravens fans, who still lamented the fact that the Colts had left Baltimore in 1984. "One guy yelled at me going off the field, 'Give us our trophies back.' I wanted to say, 'Hey, man, I was eight years old when the Colts moved out of here,'" he recalled in *Manning*.

In the final four games of the season, Manning suffered through a loss to the Atlanta Falcons, 28-21, had a good win over Cincinnati, 39-26, and then closed out the year with two losses, to Seattle and Carolina. The Indianapolis Colts went 3–13 that season and finished last in the AFC East Division. They were tied with Cincinnati and Philadelphia for the worst overall won-loss record in the entire NFL.

There was plenty of reason for disappointment, but Manning had a pretty good rookie season. He was named to the NFL All-Rookie first team by both the *Football News* and *Football Digest* and set several NFL rookie records, including completions (326), yards (3,739), and touchdown passes (26). His touchdown total was the second highest in the AFC and fourth highest in the NFL. Moreover, he had thrown more touchdown passes in his rookie season than NFL greats John Elway and Dan Marino had in 1998.

When the 1998 season ended, Manning called his father to ask if they could drive home together. Archie flew up from New Orleans, and he and Peyton talked about their experiences in the NFL. On the 13-hour drive, Archie told Peyton that a player's rookie season is the most difficult, and that the only really good thing about it was that, once it was over, it was over. Once you had played a year in the NFL, you were a veteran, and the game would begin to slow down a bit.

## MANNING AND THE NFL GREATS

One might ask: How did Peyton Manning get along with the top NFL quarterbacks and Hall of Famers? The answer, in almost every case, was . . . very well. While still a junior at Tennessee, Manning met and exchanged stories with Roger Staubach, Johnny Unitas, and John Elway. In his rookie year, he faced Dan Marino, Steve Young, and other greats on the field, and though he lost most of the encounters, he won their respect. Marino had long been Manning's favorite NFL player, and the two formed an especially close bond.

This kind of camaraderie was not the norm in the NFL, and one wonders what was different about Manning. The answer is that greats such as Elway, Marino, and Young saw the incredible potential in the young man from New Orleans, and they appreciated his dedication to the sport. They knew he might break their records one day (he has already broken some of them), but they acknowledged it as a sign that the future of the sport was bright.

The same could not be said of his relationships with other budding football greats. Later in his career, Manning squared off many times against Tom Brady of the New England Patriots, and the two superstars did not seem to get along very well. But that, too, changed over the years, as both men seemed destined to reach the Hall of Fame. Perhaps the honor of being in such a prestigious club (that of truly great quarterbacks) encouraged Manning and Brady to put aside their differences.

# The Workhorse

It is hard to say exactly when Peyton Manning became such an animated quarterback, but the transformation seemed to take place during his second season in the NFL when he began to gain more confidence. Most quarterbacks call plays in the huddle, but Manning liked to have the option of seeing how the defense was lining up against the offense before deciding to run a play. Thus, he developed a style for which he has become famous, as recounted in *Tales from the Indianapolis Colts Sideline*:

> Manning typically breaks the huddle and approaches the **line of scrimmage** with about 18 seconds remaining on the play clock. . . . He needs the time. He studies the defense. He signals and shouts. He dances up and down the line. Manning becomes an aerobics instructor, a

drum major, a disco dancer, a one-man fire drill. His calisthenics continue as the play clock ticks toward zero, and the muttering in the stands reaches full roar.

No play or system works all the time, but Manning's antics at the line of scrimmage can confuse defenders. By calling a certain play, he can see how the defense lines up and then either run the play or call a different one. It often seems that Manning is one step ahead of the defense. It goes without saying that there are times when audibling takes too much time, which may cause a delay-of-game penalty, but Manning seems to be a master at calling plays at the line of scrimmage. In 1999, he began to show just how adept he was at reading defenses and figuring out which play to call.

## THE 1999 SEASON

The 1999 season started with a game at home against the Buffalo Bills, and the Colts came out on top, 31-14. The following week, the Colts suffered a painful loss to the Patriots on the road, 31-28. But on September 26, Manning completed 29 of 54 passes for 404 yards (breaking Johnny Unitas's Colts record for passing yards in a game) as the Colts beat the San Diego Chargers, 27-19. This, his finest performance to date, showed that Manning had come of age. Next up was Miami, whom the Colts lost to in a tough one, 34-31, in a game that featured Dan Marino at his best. Passing for 393 yards, Marino showed why he was one of the all-time greats. Unfortunately, this was Marino's last year; he would retire in March 2000, having played 17 seasons in the NFL. Although the Colts had stumbled out of the gate with a 2–2 record, the loss to the Dolphins would be their last for the next 11 weeks.

The winning streak started with a 16-13 victory against the New York Jets. Then, they easily defeated Cincinnati, 31-10. They outlasted the Dallas Cowboys, 34-24, in a game that Manning threw for 313 yards. Indianapolis then beat Kansas City, 25-17, the New York Giants, 27-19, and blew out the Philadelphia Eagles, 44-17. As they rolled into the back part of their schedule, they defeated the New York Jets for the second time, 13-6, and followed that victory with a 37-34 win over the Miami Dolphins—the last time Dan Marino and Peyton Manning would square off. In the game, Marino threw for 313 yards, but Manning and the Colts were too much for Marino and the Dolphins. Indianapolis finally got a measure of revenge against New England, beating the Patriots, 20-15, on December 12. They then defeated the Washington Redskins, 24-21, and outlasted Cleveland, 29-28. There was just one game left in the regular season, a January 2 matchup with the Buffalo Bills. Used to playing in the cold weather, the Bills thrashed the Colts, 31-6. Fortunately for the Colts, they still won the AFC East and posted the second-best record in both the conference and the NFL, at 13–3—only the Jacksonville Jaguars were better, at 14–2. To top everything off, the Colts had completely reversed the previous year's record when they went 3–13. This was the greatest one-year turnaround in NFL history. *Sports Illustrated* ran a cover story on Manning in its November 22 issue. Entitled "So Good, So Soon," the article described Manning's relentless work ethic, his leadership skills, and his love for his college sweetheart, Ashley Thompson. Most important, overall, was the young man's maturity:

> His growth curve approximates the upward trajectory of one of his end-zone fade passes. "He's easily one of the top 10 quarterbacks in football, and that's a conservative statement, because there aren't ten guys I'd put ahead of him," says Fox analyst John Madden, who came away awed by Manning after working the broadcast of Indianapolis' 34-24 victory over the Dallas Cowboys on October 31. "I always had the theory that a quarterback doesn't have a clue until his fifth year, but with this guy that goes right out the window."

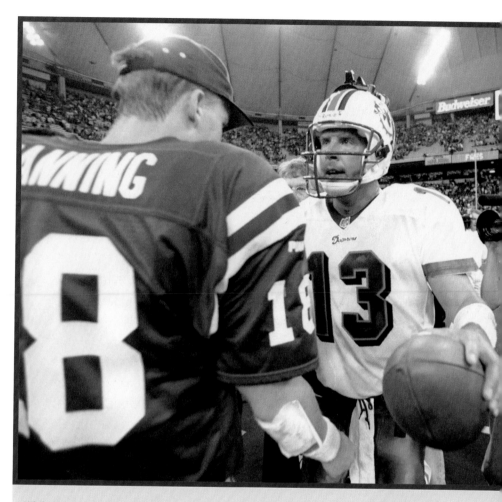

While Peyton Manning was growing up, he admired the way Dan Marino competed on the football field. Here, the two quarterbacks meet after Marino led the Miami Dolphins to a 34-31 win over Manning and the Colts on October 10, 1999. In March 2000, Marino retired from the NFL.

When John Madden speaks about football, people listen.

January 2000 was about as different from the previous January as could be imagined. In 1999, Manning had just finished his rookie season with a team that only won three games; in 2000, he was a real professional and was as well known as anyone in the game. Moreover, he had led the Colts to their best record since they moved to Indianapolis in 1984. Despite their success during the regular season, the Colts' inexperience in the playoffs showed when they hosted the Tennessee Titans in the divisional round of the AFC playoffs. Manning struggled, completing just 19 of 42 passes for 227 yards in a hard-to-swallow 19-16 loss. Despite the loss, Manning earned a trip to the Pro Bowl for the first time in his career.

## FROM BALTIMORE TO INDIANAPOLIS

Millions of older football fans—those who remember the glory days of Johnny Unitas—still associate the Colts with Baltimore. There is no way to change their mind-set, for their memories are fixed on a time when Unitas, the Colts, and the city of Baltimore were practically synonymous.

After the Colts' lease with dilapidated Memorial Stadium was up after the 1983 football season, Colts owner Robert Irsay tried to get the city of Baltimore to pay for the construction of a new stadium. Sensing that Baltimore was not going to budge, Irsay began talking to officials from other cities about possibly relocating. He also feared that Baltimore officials might use the principle of eminent domain to seize the Colts and make them stay in the city that loved them so much. Then came a fateful night in March 1984. In the dead of night, several moving trucks arrived at the Colts' training facility, and after movers packed all the equipment, the team headed west to Indianapolis. Negotiations with Indianapolis mayor William Hudnut had been ongoing for some time, and Irsay seized the moment to depart. Unfortunately, he left behind thousands of grieving, and sometimes angry, fans.

The 2000 football season was upon Manning before he knew it, and like every other successful NFL player, he was expected to do even better than the year before. This put quite a bit of pressure on Manning, but he was up for the challenge. During his career, Manning made a point of saying that there are no breaks given, no corners cut, in the NFL. One earns one's place every day, or falls by the wayside.

Resettling in Indianapolis, the Colts had a hard time re-establishing their image. The team won a total of 12 games in their first three years in Indianapolis. They then fielded a competitive squad for the next few years, before posting an abysmal 1–15 record in 1991. Robert Irsay acquired the reputation of being a strange, moody man, and the Colts organization started to fall apart. But in the autumn of 1997, nearly 14 years after his father had moved the organization, Jim Irsay (who took over after his father's death earlier that year) fired Vice President and Director of Football Operations Bill Tobin and Coach Lindy Infante, and began to reshape the Indianapolis Colts into the team they are today. The Colts were fortunate in that they finished 3–13 in 1997, which gave them the number-one pick in the 1998 NFL draft.

After the Colts drafted Peyton Manning, they began to surround him with talented players and then added the final piece of the puzzle in 2002, when they hired Tony Dungy as head coach. By this time, the Colts organization was the strongest it had ever been, and the team was on the verge of doing something special.

## THE 2000 SEASON

Indianapolis opened the 2000 season with a good win on the road against the Kansas City Chiefs, beating them, 27-14. From there, the Colts hosted the Oakland Raiders. Even though Manning completed 33 of 48 passes for 367 yards, the Colts lost to the Raiders, 38-31. Just in his third season, Manning was routinely throwing for more yards than any other quarterback in the NFL.

Then came an appearance on Monday Night Football. The Colts hosted the Jacksonville Jaguars in a showdown that pitted the teams with the best regular-season records the previous year. Manning sparkled on the national stage, completing 23 of 36 passes for a career-high and franchise-record 440 yards and four touchdowns in a convincing 43-14 win. If he continued to torch defenses like this, he would soon be recognized as one of the greatest quarterbacks of all time!

Next up was a trip to Buffalo to try to get revenge for the disappointing loss at the end of the 1999 season. In a defensive struggle in which Manning only threw for 187 yards, the Colts got by the Bills, 18-16. The following week, the Colts lost to the Patriots, 24-16, even though Manning threw for 334 yards. Indianapolis then went on a three-game tear, beating the Seattle Seahawks, the Patriots, and the Detroit Lions. The Colts then lost to the Chicago Bears, 27-24, despite another 300-yard game by Manning; beat the New York Jets, 23-15; and then traveled to Green Bay for what was billed as one of the great matchups between two of the best quarterbacks in the NFL: Peyton Manning and Brett Favre.

Like Manning, Favre was from the South, but the similarities ended there. Favre was from rural Mississippi and was quite brash. He was a gunslinger and tended to rely too much on his arm strength, which often resulted in interceptions. Manning was the more measured quarterback, choosing his passes more carefully. Favre got the best of Manning in this,

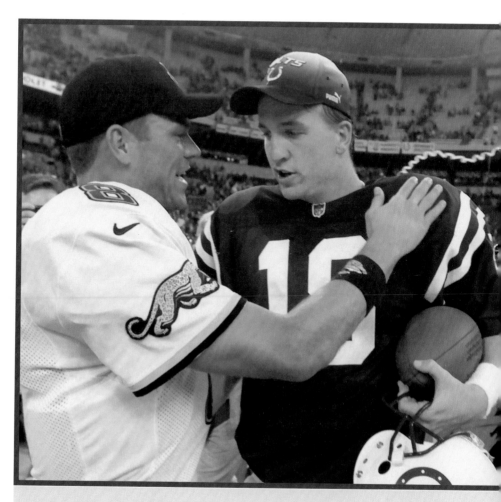

In his first appearance on Monday Night Football, Peyton Manning made quite an impression: He completed 23 of 36 passes for a career-high and franchise-record 440 yards and four touchdowns in a 43-14 win over the Jacksonville Jaguars on September 25, 2000. Here, Jaguars quarterback Mark Brunell congratulates Manning after his record-setting performance.

their first meeting, 26-24. During the coming years, the two quarterbacks would each take their place among the pantheon of NFL greats, and experts and fans alike often argue which quarterback is better.

Next came a loss to Miami, 17-14, and another to the New York Jets, 27-17. However, the Colts closed out the year in fine form, beating Buffalo, Miami, and Minnesota. Despite their 10–6 record, the Colts finished behind the Dolphins in the AFC East, and the two teams were set to meet in the first round of the playoffs. Although Manning and the Colts had a 14-point lead at halftime, thanks in part to three Dolphins **turnovers**, Miami stormed back in the second half to tie the game at 17 with just 34 seconds left in the contest. The Colts

## IRON MEN OF THE NFL

At the time this book was written, there was absolutely no doubt Brett Favre was the true "Iron Man" of the NFL. And although his record for consecutive games played by a quarterback is impressive, there is another quarterback who could conceivably catch him if he plays long enough—Peyton Manning.

Born in Mississippi in 1969, Favre is seven years older than Manning. He was drafted by the Atlanta Falcons in 1991 (seven years before Manning as well) and then traded to the Green Bay Packers the following year. Favre started 13 games as the team's quarterback in 1992. Since then, he has never relinquished the starting spot and has never missed a game during the last 16 seasons! Through the 2007 regular season, he had played in a total of 277 NFL games (including playoff games) of which he had been the starting quarterback in *273 in a row*! There has never been another quarterback—not even in the glory days of the iron men of the 1940s and 1950s—who has come close to achieving this feat.

missed a field-goal attempt in overtime, and the Dolphins finished them off with a long drive that ended in a 17-yard touchdown run by Miami **tailback** Lamar Smith. Once again, Manning struggled in the 23-17 loss, completing just 17 of 32 passes for 194 yards. Despite the disappointing loss, Manning had an excellent year overall; he threw 33 touchdown passes (to lead the AFC and tie for first place in the NFL overall), and he threw for a total of 4,413 yards, best in the NFL.

Born in New Orleans in 1976, Manning came to the NFL in 1998. Perhaps with the exception of Favre, Manning's statistical accomplishments are incomparable. Like Favre, he has played with the same team and started every single game of his career. The only difference is that Favre has missed several **snaps** due to injury, while Manning has only missed one snap after he had to leave a game against the Dolphins in 2001 because of a broken jaw. Even then, he returned for the next game. Through the 2007 regular season, Manning had played in 160 NFL games and started *160 of them in a row!*

Can Manning catch Favre some day and surpass his amazing record? It is similar to asking if Buzz Aldrin and Neil Armstrong (to use an analogy from the space program) should have stepped out of the lunar module at the same moment and been the first men on the moon at the same time. Like the first men to step on the moon, Manning and Favre are in a class all their own.

On March 17, 2001, Peyton Manning and his long-time girlfriend, Ashley Thompson, got married in Memphis, Tennessee. The couple is pictured here during a trip to the White House in May 2007.

## MARRIAGE

Manning took the loss to Miami as he did almost all other losses—not very well. His older brother, Cooper, once said he would not call Peyton for a solid week after most losses. But at the beginning of 2001, Manning had other things on his mind, specifically his wedding.

Manning and Ashley Thompson had first met in 1993. She grew up in Memphis, the daughter of a successful businessman who had ties to the University of Tennessee football program. The Thompsons had hosted Manning briefly during his senior year in high school, and Peyton and Ashley quickly became fond of one another.

Despite the fact that Ashley attended the University of Virginia, the couple dated throughout their college years. Knowing she wanted to stay with Peyton after they graduated, Ashley planned her career (she graduated with a degree in finance and marketing and is a real estate developer) so they could be together. None of the temptations that might have moved another man had any effect on Peyton, who declared early on that Ashley was his one and only. The couple got married in Memphis on March 17, 2001. By then, Manning had firmly settled in Indianapolis, not only in a career sense but also as a homeowner. Ashley moved into his large home in the city, and the Southern couple delighted in becoming—at least as far as their friends were concerned—Northerners!

# The Rivalry

For two men who were both so passionate about football, Tom Brady and Peyton Manning could hardly have been more different. It is true that they are about the same height and that they were both used to winning on the football field, but the two come from quite different backgrounds and they approach the game differently. One could almost say they came from different ends of the American spectrum.

Born and raised in New Orleans, Manning was reared to be a Southern gentleman, mighty in deeds and sparing in words (he had overcome the latter part of that training rather well). Born and raised in suburban San Francisco, Brady exuded a California-style carelessness but did so in a very endearing way.

Groomed first by his father, and then by the coaches at Isidore Newman High School and the University of

Tennessee, Manning had great potential from the start, a potential that was recognized by family, friends, and coaches. Conversely, Tom Brady was the number-three quarterback at the University of Michigan, overshadowed by Brian Griese, the son of legendary Miami Dolphins quarterback Bob Griese. But "Tom Terrific," as many called him, worked his way up the ladder.

Manning was the top pick in the 1998 NFL draft; Brady was selected in the sixth round of the 2000 NFL draft (the 199th player overall). He was drafted by the New England Patriots, who have thanked their lucky stars ever since.

Brady came to New England in 2000, but he did not become the team's starting quarterback until the autumn of 2001, when veteran quarterback Drew Bledsoe suffered an injury against the New York Jets during the second game of the season. Within a matter of weeks, Brady became the acknowledged leader of the Patriots. His loose and easygoing personality was balanced by his fierce desire to win, which made him a crowd favorite. He also was fortunate to be coached by one of the best in the business, Bill Belichick.

Tom Brady and Peyton Manning met for the first time (on the field, at least) in the third game of the 2001 regular season. Manning was then entering his fourth season, and Brady was playing in his second game, after relieving Bledsoe the week before. The New England Patriots took that game, 44-13, and won a rematch two weeks later, 38-17, even though Manning passed for 335 yards that day. Suddenly, it seemed, the Indianapolis Colts faced a defense that could neutralize their potent offense.

## MANNING'S ROUGH YEAR

At the beginning of the 2001 season, no one expected Manning or the Colts to go through a rough spell; they had gone 10–6 the previous year, and Manning had clearly established

# THE "NEW" NEW ENGLAND PATRIOTS

For much of their history, they had been one of the laugh-ingstocks of the NFL. The Patriots had always had talent and sometimes they had come close to greatness, but they always seemed to falter in the crucial moments. They had reached the Super Bowl in 1986, only to be blown out by the Chicago Bears, 46-10. Under fiery coach Bill Parcells, they reached the Super Bowl in 1997, only to be manhandled by the Green Bay Packers, 35-21. But in 2000, Bill Belichick, one of Bill Parcells's former assistant coaches, became head coach, and the Patriots quickly became one of the NFL's elite teams.

In a time of showy coaches and even showier players (one thinks of the endless dances and gyrations in the **end zone**), Belichick came across as the ultimate working-class coach. Wearing a hooded sweatshirt and showing a no-nonsense atti-tude, Belichick became one of the hardest-working coaches in the NFL. He expected his players to work equally hard, and, with the exception of Tom Brady, the Patriots were not a team of superstars. Their success seemed to come from a team spirit and overall desire to win.

Belichick coached the Patriots to victory in Super Bowls XXXVI (a 20-17 win over the St. Louis Rams), XXXVIII (a 32-29 win over the Carolina Panthers), and XXXIX (a 24-21 win over the Philadelphia Eagles). Each game was seen, by commenta-tors, as vindication of an old-style coaching philosophy mixed with a brand-new level of sophistication in defensive prepara-tion (both personified by Belichick). Much to the surprise of fans throughout the country, the Patriots became the darlings of the new millennium, and the team to beat.

himself as one of the best quarterbacks in the NFL. But something went wrong as the Colts entered the middle part of their 2001 schedule. After rebounding to win two in a row after the second loss to New England, the Colts went into a tailspin. First they lost to Miami, 27-24, then they fell, 34-20, to a 4–4 New Orleans team.

But that was only the beginning. The next week, they got blasted by the 49ers, 40-21, despite 370 yards passing by Manning. That loss was followed by a 39-27 defeat at the hands of the Baltimore Ravens. Finally, they dropped their fifth game in a row; an embarrassing 41-6 loss to Miami on Monday Night Football. Indianapolis looked so bad that commentators began to talk about Manning and the Colts as if the 1999 and 2000 seasons had been an aberration. At this point, the Colts were 4–8 and struggling to keep their heads above water.

Although they rebounded with a 41-27 win over the Atlanta Falcons, they dropped their next two games, to the New York Jets, 29-28, and to the St. Louis Rams, 42-17. The Colts got a measure of revenge in the last regular-season game when they pounded Denver, 29-10, but the overall results were disheartening, to say the least. Indianapolis went 6–10 in 2001, ensuring that they would finish in fourth place in their last season in the AFC East Division.

Part of the trouble was easy to diagnose. Star running back Edgerrin James tore his ACL (anterior cruciate ligament) in the sixth game of the season against Kansas City and was out for the rest of the year. But the magnitude of the losses, to Miami especially, was hard to explain away. The blame largely fell on the shoulders of the defense, which gave up the most points (486) in a season by an NFL team since 1981. Something had gone wrong with the mighty Colts machine. Then came a break, one that everyone in Indianapolis was looking for.

On September 30, 2001, New England Patriots quarterback Tom Brady and Peyton Manning squared off for the first time in their careers. Here, Manning dejectedly walks off the field during the first quarter of the 44-13 loss. In the game, Manning threw for just 196 yards and was intercepted three times. During the next four years, the Colts would lose six straight games to the Patriots.

## COACH DUNGY

Over in the NFC, Coach Tony Dungy had guided the Tampa Bay Buccaneers (a team that had been a laughingstock for years) to four playoff appearances in his six years as head coach. (Dungy's first playoff team in 1997 was the franchise's first since 1982.) Unfortunately for Dungy, he could not get the Buccaneers to the Super Bowl, and after his team was unceremoniously dumped by the Philadelphia Eagles, 31-9, in the 2001 playoffs, he was fired. Indianapolis Colts owner Robert Irsay jumped at the chance to hire a coach with such a great track record.

Dungy did not come cheap; his initial five-year contract cost the Colts $13 million. When questioned about Dungy's salary, and about his decision to hire him, Irsay replied, "You have to pay for greatness. This was too important a decision for the franchise to not get this done." This turned out to be one of the times when a big expenditure was indeed justified by the results.

Born in Michigan in 1955, Dungy had already "been around" the NFL a long time. After playing quarterback for the University of Minnesota, he signed as a free agent with the Pittsburgh Steelers in 1977. Unfortunately for Dungy, the Steelers had a Pro Bowl quarterback in Terry Bradshaw. In addition, it was also a time when black quarterbacks were often moved to another position when they reached the NFL, so Dungy ended up playing **safety** and on **special teams** during his short NFL career. He played two years for Pittsburgh and one year with the San Francisco 49ers before being cut. He then decided to get into coaching and began his career at his alma mater, where he coached **defensive backs**. At the time, it was also difficult for African Americans to enter the NFL coaching ranks, but the Steelers hired him as a defensive coach in 1981. He worked his way up the ranks and became the league's youngest defensive coordinator in 1984. Then, after stints as the defensive backs coach for the Kansas City Chiefs and defensive coordinator for the Minnesota Vikings, Dungy finally got the opportunity to be a head coach when the Tampa Bay Buccaneers hired him in 1996. (This was only seven years after Art Shell became the first African-American NFL head coach in 1989.) During his six seasons in Tampa, Dungy's teams consistently had one of the top defenses in the NFL. In addition to making the Buccaneers a perennial playoff contender, Dungy was the most successful coach in franchise history: During his six-year tenure, the Buccaneers went 54–42 in the regular season, compared to a 43–111 record the 10 seasons prior to his arrival.

Because the Colts already had a high-scoring offense, it made perfect sense to hire a coach who specialized in defense. Dungy decided not to tamper with the Colts' offense; instead he focused on installing his "Tampa 2" defense. On January 22, 2002, Dungy was named the Colts' ninth head coach since the team had moved to Indianapolis in 1984. The times were about to change.

## PEYTON'S OFFENSE, TONY'S DEFENSE

By 2002, when Dungy arrived as head coach, Peyton Manning had already become the unofficial leader of the Indianapolis Colts. By virtue of his relentless work ethic and determination to succeed, Manning had evolved into a well-respected player.

Some people may have expected that the offensive-minded Manning and the defensive-minded Dungy would clash. But the two men got along well right from the start, partly because they had one goal: to win a Super Bowl. By then Manning had become a true student of the game; perhaps studying more game film than any other player in the NFL. During his playing days, Dungy had also spent a good deal of time in the film room. Both men believed in being well prepared. As Manning said in *Tales from the Indianapolis Colts Sideline*:

> Tony's in our meetings all the time. I believe he's in our offensive meetings more than he is in the defensive meetings. He sits in the back. He chimes in. He's very vocal. You hear the door close and he's back with the defense, but a little later he comes back to our meeting.

The 2002 NFL season started with a road game against division foe Jacksonville. (With the addition of the expansion Houston Texans prior to the 2002 season, the Colts, Tennessee Titans, Jacksonville Jaguars, and Texans formed the new AFC South Division.) The Colts edged the Jaguars, 28-25. The next week, the Colts dropped their fifth straight game to the Miami Dolphins at the RCA Dome, 21-13. But the Colts rebounded to win their next three games, beating the expansion Houston Texans, 23-3; the 0–5 Cincinnati Bengals, 28-21; and the Baltimore Ravens, 22-20, which gave them a 4–1 record—tied for the best start since the franchise moved to Indianapolis. Then came an appearance on Monday Night Football.

Debuting in 1970, Monday Night Football had become the showcase game for the NFL—a three-hour spectacle on the first work night of every week, a time when players could showcase their talents in front of a national television audience. Manning passed for 304 yards that night, but threw three interceptions, including one that was returned for a touchdown, in a 28-10 loss to the Pittsburgh Steelers. That was followed by a 26-21 loss to the Washington Redskins and a painful defeat at the hands of AFC South rival Tennessee, 23-15. Manning completed 37 of 50 passes for 327 yards against the Titans, but the Colts fell to 4–4 at the halfway point of the season. With a playoff appearance seemingly slipping through their hands, the Colts had to make a run.

And that was exactly what they did. They defeated Philadelphia, 35-13; Dallas, 20-3; Denver, 23-20; and Houston, 19-3, to bring an 8–4 record into a crucial AFC South rematch with Tennessee. However, the four-game roll was halted by the Titans, 27-17. Despite throwing for 297 yards, Manning was intercepted three times, as the Colts fell to 0–10 when he threw at least three interceptions in a game. The Colts rebounded to beat the Browns, 28-23, as Manning threw for 277 yards, 172 of which went to his favorite target, wide receiver Marvin Harrison. But the Colts could not keep the momentum, losing to the New York Giants, 44-27, despite Manning's 365 yards passing. By virtue of their 20-13 victory over Jacksonville, the Colts finished 10–6 and earned the fifth seed in the AFC play-offs, where they would face off against the fourth-seeded New York Jets. No one had to tell Manning that winning either of the two regular-season games against Tennessee would have made the Colts AFC South Division champions. But the team did not, so they had to prepare for a road game against the Jets. Although most observers believed the Colts had a good chance of winning the contest, it would turn out to be one of the most embarrassing losses of Manning's career.

Manning completed only 14 of 31 passes for 137 yards, and the entire Colts offense produced only 176 yards in a humiliat-ing 41-0 loss. It was the first time since Manning had become quarterback in 1998 (83 games) that the Colts had failed to score. It also was his second-lowest passing total since he entered the league and his lowest **passer rating** (31.2).

Peyton Manning, whose overall statistics indicated he was one of the best quarterbacks of all time, was now 0–3 in post-season play. And that was not the end of it. Colts kicker Mike Vanderjagt was generally considered one of the most important players on the team; he was probably the single most consistent field goal kicker in the NFL. But Vanderjagt also had a big mouth, and the day after losing to the Jets, he criticized both Coach Dungy and Manning, as recounted in *Tales from the Indianapolis Colts Sideline*:

> I think you need a motivator. I think you need a guy that is going to get in somebody's face when they're not per-forming well enough. Manning and Tony [Dungy] are basically the same guy. They work hard; they mark their Xs and Os and go out and execute. If it doesn't happen, there's nothing we can do about it. . . . I'm not a real big Colts fan right now. I just don't see us getting better.

In Peyton Manning's third career playoff appearance, the Indianapolis Colts were soundly defeated by the New York Jets, 41-0. Manning completed just 14 of 31 passes for 137 yards, and many pundits began to wonder if he had what it took to win a big game. Here, Manning is sacked by Jets defensive end John Abraham during the second quarter of the January 4, 2003, game.

Coach Dungy was disturbed by the kicker's comments, but Manning was furious. Asked about Vanderjagt's comments, Manning replied that the "idiot kicker" had spoiled his own reputation and that of other kickers, too. But the issue had to be resolved, for it could have caused a rift in the organization. Both men apologized, and the incident seemed to go away, though it was not far from anyone's memory.

## THE 2003 SEASON

The Colts started the 2003 season with a five-game winning streak, despite a disappointing first game. They opened up on the road, beating Cleveland, 9-6, in what was one of the lowest-scoring games in recent Colts history. From there the Colts hoped to get a measure of revenge against the Tennessee Titans, the defending AFC South Division champions and a team that had yet to lose to the Colts since the franchise moved from Houston in 1997. They did just that, dismantling the Titans, 33-7, behind 120 yards rushing by running back Edgerrin James. Next, the Colts hosted Jacksonville. Despite being down 3-0 at halftime, Indianapolis outscored Jacksonville 23-10 in the second half to win, 23-13. The Colts then headed out on the road for two games against NFC South Division teams. First, they thrashed the New Orleans Saints, 55-21, in a game that Manning completed 20 of 25 passes for 314 yards and a career-high and Colts record six touchdowns. Marvin Harrison led the way with six catches for 158 yards and three touchdowns. The Colts carried a 4–0 record to Tampa Bay, for the first meeting between Coach Dungy and his former team. What resulted was a classic Monday Night Football contest, generally considered one of the most compelling games ever played.

Tampa Bay came out swinging, and they connected beautifully in the first 30 minutes. The Buccaneers scored two touchdowns in the first quarter and added a third in the second, to jump out to a 21-0 halftime lead. The statistics alone, however, do not tell the whole story. Tampa Bay had won the

Super Bowl eight months earlier, and they played like world champions. Not only did the Buccaneers have a magnificent defense, but their offense was clicking on all cylinders. Monday Night Football analyst John Madden (the former coach of the Oakland Raiders) thought Tampa Bay's first half was one of the best performances he had ever seen. The Buccaneers had racked up 239 yards in the first half, including 189 through the air in taking the commanding three-touchdown lead.

Tampa Bay and Indianapolis traded touchdowns in the third quarter, making the score 28-7. That 21-point lead was not insurmountable, not with 15 minutes to play, but it was a steep hill to climb. Manning came out throwing at the start of the fourth quarter. He made good throws to Reggie Wayne and Marvin Harrison before Ricky Williams scored on a one-yard touchdown run, making it 28-14 with only 12 minutes to go. However, Manning then made a huge mistake that appeared to be costly. On third-and-15 from his own 11-yard line, he threw an interception to Tampa cornerback Ronde Barber, who returned it 29 yards for a touchdown and a 35-14 lead with just 5:22 left in the game. "That seals the deal," said John Madden (no one disagreed).

It was at about this time in the game that Madden said he had spoken with an NFL player just the other day, and that, when asked whom he would like to have as quarterback in such a tight situation, his choice would be Peyton Manning. Madden's comment would prove prophetic. This was Manning's chance to prove himself. His determination was obvious, but first he had to navigate the tough Tampa Bay defense.

Feeling the game was theirs, Tampa Bay kicker Martin Gramatica booted the kickoff two yards deep into the end zone. Colts kick returner Brad Pyatt gathered the ball and then took off down the field for a 90-yard return all the way to the Tampa 12-yard line. On the strength of two James Mungro runs, the Colts punched it in with just 3:43 left in the game. John Madden said, "Indianapolis is still alive," but he was quick to follow up with the observation that no team in NFL history had overcome a three-touchdown deficit with less than four minutes remaining in the game.

But then Colts kicker Mike Vanderjagt pulled off a remarkable onside kick that gave them the ball at their own 42. Coming in once more, Manning made one good throw for 15 yards, then a better one to Marvin Harrison to get the Colts down to the Buccaneers' 32-yard line. Operating from the **shotgun**, Manning then hit Marvin Harrison with a 28-yard touchdown pass that pulled the Colts to within seven at 35-28, with just 2:38 left. The touchdown pass set a franchise record: Manning and Harrison had now hooked up on 64 career touchdowns, surpassing the record of 63 set by Johnny Unitas and Raymond Berry, who played together from 1956 to 1967.

The Colts then lined up for another onside kick. This time Tampa Bay recovered the ball, but they could do little with it. After no gain on **first down**, the Colts called their last time out. On second down, the Buccaneers actually lost two yards, then were hit with an unnecessary roughness penalty, and came up short on third down. Indianapolis and Manning would get the ball one more time. Tampa Bay **punted** and the Colts took over at their own 15. John Madden again posed his question, one that was becoming rhetorical: "Who would you want in this situation?" The answer was obvious.

Manning threw his first pass away in a hurry, then found wide receiver Troy Walters for a 12-yard gain to bring his team to the 27-yard line. In addition, Tampa defensive lineman Warren Sapp was called for roughing the passer, which moved the Colts out to their own 42 with 1:37 left in the game. Manning followed this with a spectacular 52-yard throw to Harrison who got the ball to Tampa Bay's 6-yard line. Two plays later, Williams punched the ball over the **goal line**, and when the **extra point** was good, Indianapolis had tied the game at 35, with just 38 seconds left in regulation, setting the stage for overtime.

Tampa Bay won the coin toss and elected to receive. Quarterback Brad Johnson and the Buccaneers got into Colts territory but not close enough to try a field goal. Eventually Tampa Bay punted, and Manning got the ball on his own 13-yard line. His first pass was tipped and **incomplete**. On second down, the Colts gained four yards on the ground. Then, on third-and-six, Manning hit Harrison yet again, to bring the Colts up to their own 25-yard line.

After a couple of unsuccessful plays, Manning hit Reggie Wayne for 16 yards on third-and-11. He then converted another third-down play by completing a pass to Troy Walters to get the Colts into Buccaneers territory. There was another overthrow, but then Manning delivered a pass to Wayne at the Tampa Bay 31-yard line. At this point, John Madden commented, "The freshest guy [on the field] looks like Peyton Manning." Running back James Mungro then carried the ball three straight times for nine yards to set the Colts up for a field-goal attempt. Kicker Mike Vanderjagt, who was 12 for 12 on the season and had converted 86 percent of his kicks during his NFL career, trotted onto the field to attempt a 40-yarder. This was the moment!

Vanderjagt's kick was . . . no good! The Buccaneers were about to get the ball back when the officials ruled that Tampa **defensive end** Simeon Rice had been caught "leaping" during the attempt to block the field goal and thus was charged with a 15-yard unsportsmanlike penalty. Amidst much confusion on the field, the officials stood by their call, and Vanderjagt got another chance. This time his kick was deflected, hit the right upright, and then went through for three points and the end to one of the wackiest and most intense games ever seen on Monday Night Football. Manning and the Colts had won, 38-35, and they had made Tony Dungy proud. He had beaten his old team at Raymond James Stadium, and to top it all off, he had done so on his birthday!

Peyton Manning and Indianapolis head coach Tony Dungy walk off the field together after the Colts' stunning 38-35 overtime win over the Tampa Bay Buccaneers on October 6, 2003. The victory was particularly satisfying for Dungy, who had coached the Buccaneers from 1996 to 2001, but was fired for his inability to get Tampa Bay to the Super Bowl.

Sporting a 5–0 record for the first time since 1977, the Colts returned to Indianapolis, where they were promptly knocked off by the undefeated Carolina Panthers, 23-20. But then they came back to post back-to-back wins over Houston, 30-21, and Miami, 23-17. A painful loss at Jacksonville came next, with the Jaguars winning, 28-23, in a game that Manning passed for 347 yards. (By now, a 300-plus-yard day was becoming almost routine!) Indianapolis then hosted the Jets, whom they hoped to pay back for the humiliating loss they suffered in the first round of the playoffs the year before. Although they did not dominate the game, they won, 38-31, behind Manning, who completed 27 of 36 passes for 401 yards, and James, who rushed for 127 yards to become the Colts' all-time leading rusher. The following week, the Colts traveled to Buffalo, where they beat the Bills, 17-14. Then the Colts stumbled against the team that was becoming their nemesis: the New England Patriots. Despite a four-touchdown game by Manning, the Colts could not overcome a 31-10 third-quarter deficit and dropped a 38-34 decision, giving Tom Brady and his Patriots a 4-0 lead in head-to-head games with Manning and the Colts.

In Week 14, the Colts beat the Tennessee Titans, 29-27, for their second win over their AFC South Division rival that season. Next up was quarterback Michael Vick and the Atlanta Falcons. The Colts frustrated Vick all day, sacking him four times and holding him to just 77 yards of total offense in a 38-7 smackdown. These victories were followed by a disappointing 31-17 loss to the Denver Broncos, which delayed the Colts from winning the AFC South Division title. Fortunately, they wrapped up the title for the first time in franchise history with a 20-17 win over Houston to finish the regular season 12–4.

## POSTSEASON VICTORY

Heading into the playoffs after the 2003 season, Manning and the Colts were 0–3 in postseason play. No one doubted the resolve of Manning, Coach Dungy, or the team, but there seemed to be a hex on Indianapolis when it came to postseason play. Knowing that they had to get the proverbial monkey off their back, the Colts staged a big performance when they hosted the Denver Broncos at the RCA Dome in the first round of the playoffs.

Manning and the Colts scored first, on a 31-yard pass to wide receiver Brandon Stokley. Denver came back with a field goal, but Manning connected with Marvin Harrison for a 46-yard touchdown, and soon it became a rout, with Indianapolis scoring 14 points in the first quarter, 17 points in the second, and 10 points in the third. Final score: 41-10. Manning's wife, Ashley, claimed she had never seen him so relaxed before a big game. *Sports Illustrated* praised Manning and noted his outstanding performance:

> In the best game of his six-year career—hell, in the best game of almost anyone's career—Manning was composed, confident and in command. He connected on 22 of 26 passes for 377 yards (327 by halftime) and five touchdowns.

One week later, on January 11, the Colts went to Arrowhead Stadium to play the Kansas City Chiefs in an AFC divisional playoff game. The Chiefs had won 13 games in a row at home, partly because of their inspired and noisy fans. Edgerrin James, who by then had fully recovered from his torn ACL, remembered in *Tales from the Indianapolis Colts Sideline* that it was at Arrowhead where he had suffered his career-threatening injury. Was he nervous about getting hurt again?

> I'm not superstitious. . . . It's a football game. [The injury] is one of those things that was unfortunate, but it's part of the game. It's cool. The last time you go there, things didn't work out. Now, you're going back and there's more on the line.

The Colts grabbed an early 14-3 lead, but Kansas City came back in the second and third quarters. Neither the Colts nor the Chiefs punted in the game—the first time that had happened in

NFL playoff history. Despite the fact that the Colts did not have an offensive penalty and converted 8 of 11 third downs, they could never fully take control of the game because their defense struggled at times. Although the Chiefs cut the Colts' lead to seven, at 38-31, with just 4:22 left, the Colts were able to salt away the game with an eight-play drive that lasted more than four minutes. Manning had another wonderful game, completing 22 of 30 passes for 304 yards and three touchdowns. And what about Edgerrin James? He rushed 26 times for a career-playoff-best 125 yards.

Curses, it seemed, were meant to be broken.

## LOST CHAMPIONSHIP

The following week, the Colts went to Gillette Stadium in Foxborough, Massachusetts, to play the New England Patriots for the AFC Championship. Statistically, the game favored the Colts, whose offense was the most explosive in the NFL. But Bill Belichick and the Patriots were prepared.

Michael Silver of *Sports Illustrated* described the game in his story entitled "Cold Blooded," which appeared in the January 24, 2004, issue of the magazine:

> As always, the blueprint conceived by New England coach Bill Belichick and his brainy defensive coordinator, Romeo Crennel, contained more wrinkles than a Rolling Stones jet tour. Reasoning that Manning does not throw as well when he can't set his feet and step into his throws, the Pats' twin wizards came up with a 4-2-5 nickel alignment that would pressure Manning by featuring back-up defensive end Jarvis Green as a second **tackle** alongside mammoth veteran Ted Washington.

New England quarterback Tom Brady put it much more succinctly. The week before meeting the Colts, he watched as Manning and his team put up 38 points against the Kansas

City Chiefs but realized that, in giving up 31 points, they were vulnerable. As recounted in *Sports Illustrated*, Brady said to his sister, "We're going to kill these guys this time. Trust me."

Indeed, Tom Terrific had his way, as he completed 22 of 37 passes for 237 yards. Although Manning also threw for 237 yards, he tossed four interceptions, including one in the end zone as the Colts were driving for a touchdown. The Patriots went on to win, 24-14, and advance to the Super Bowl, where they beat the Carolina Panthers, 32-29. Those who followed the Manning-Brady rivalry observed that Manning could put more points on the board—and in a hurry, too—than anyone else in the game, but that Brady was steady under pressure and thrived in the big game. Despite coming up short, Manning was named NFL co-MVP (with Steve McNair) after throwing for a league-high 4,267 yards and 29 touchdowns and leading the Colts to their best season record (14–5) since 1968.

# Best Man,
# No Ring

Everyone knows that the best man is intended to bring the bride's ring to the wedding and to hand it to the groom at the most important moment. During the 2002 and 2003 seasons, there was little doubt Peyton Manning had become the best at what he did (throwing touchdowns), but he was unable to win the big game and claim that elusive Super Bowl ring.

## THE MAGIC SEASON

The 2004 NFL season featured a number of talented quarterbacks, sprinkled throughout the league. Manning had the best numbers to that point, but Daunte Culpepper of the Minnesota Vikings and Ben Roethlisberger of the Pittsburgh Steelers were coming on strong. Then, too, old standout Brett Favre started off strong for his best season in many years.

The Colts started where the previous season left off—in New England—where they dropped a disappointing game, 27-24, against the Patriots. Not only did New England win, but this was one of the rare occasions where Manning was outperformed by another quarterback—Brady passed for 335 yards to Manning's 256 that day. Even with a potent offense and an improving defense, Indianapolis could not cope with the variety of surprises that Patriots coach Bill Belichick threw at them. After losing the season opener, the Colts traveled to Nashville, where they beat the Tennessee Titans, 31-17, before returning home to face Green Bay in a shootout between Manning and Packers quarterback Brett Favre. This was a classic meeting of the NFL's two "Iron Men": Favre had not missed a start since 1992, and Manning had not missed a start since 1998. Favre showed much of his old magic, throwing for 360 yards, but Manning outdid him, completing 28 of 40 passes for 393 yards, including 320 in the first half, and five touchdowns. The Colts took the game, 45-31. Beating Favre and the Packers at the RCA Dome showed that Manning's fine numbers from the previous year (and his remarkable comeback against Tampa Bay) were no fluke.

Just a week after the big matchup with Favre, Manning celebrated a milestone. The game between Indianapolis and the Jacksonville Jaguars was his one hundredth start in a row—at this rate, he might even equal Favre's consecutive games streak someday. The Colts took the game, 24-17, then returned home to beat the Oakland Raiders, 35-14, behind 136 yards rushing from Edgerrin James.

After a bye week, Manning and the Colts hosted Jacksonville, in a game filled with errors. The Colts committed 12 penalties—the most by the team in 113 games—and fumbled the ball twice in a disappointing 27-24 loss. Manning completed 27 of 39 passes for 368 yards that day, but it was not enough. The following week, at Kansas City, he completed 25 of 44 passes for 472 yards (a career best) and five touchdowns against the

During the 2004 season, Peyton Manning and Brett Favre squared off in an epic duel. When all was said and done, Manning had completed 28 of 40 passes for 393 yards and five touchdowns, while Favre completed 30 of 44 passes for 360 yards and four touchdowns. In all, the two teams combined for 912 yards of offense, but the Colts got the better of the Packers, 45-31. Here, Manning and Favre congratulate each other after the game.

Chiefs, only to come up on the losing end of a 45-35 score. The Colts' defense gave up an astonishing 590 yards (the most in 35 years) in the loss.

In Week 9, the Colts entertained the Minnesota Vikings in a Monday Night Football matchup that pitted the league's top two quarterbacks that season. Indianapolis scraped by in this game, winning 31-28, behind 268 yards passing from Manning. In addition, Harrison and Manning broke the NFL record for career completions between a quarterback and wide receiver with 664. Although Vikings quarterback Daunte Culpepper threw for a season-low 169 yards, the 2004 season was his best as a pro, as he passed for a league-leading 4,717 yards and a franchise-record 39 touchdowns. At the time, the Colts' win did not look very impressive, but it was the start of an eight-game winning streak that would propel them to their second-straight AFC South Division title. The Colts beat the Houston Texans, 49-14, the Chicago Bears, 41-10, and the Detroit Lions, 41-9. Manning often sat out parts of the fourth quarter of these games, for there was no need to overuse him during these easy wins. Meanwhile, his overall numbers, especially those for touchdown passes and yards gained, were bringing him ever closer to breaking an all-time record in those categories, set by one of his heroes. In fact, in the win over Detroit, Manning threw six touchdown passes, one short of the NFL single-game record.

In the Colts' twelfth game, Manning completed 25 of 33 passes for 425 yards in a 51-24 blowout win over the Tennessee Titans. Indianapolis continued its winning ways in December, beating the Houston Texans yet again, 23-14, and then defeating the Baltimore Ravens, 20-10. At this point, Manning was within one touchdown pass of equaling the all-time record of 48 set by Dolphins quarterback Dan Marino in 1984. Some commentators thought this record would never be broken, but suddenly Manning was knocking at the door.

Michael Silver of *Sports Illustrated* declared that Manning was up to the task:

> Now chew on this. No NFL passer, not even the great Marino, has had as productive a season as Manning's magical 2004 campaign seems destined to turn out. On Sunday at Reliant Stadium, Manning threw a pair

of first-quarter touchdown passes to lead Indianapolis to a 23-14 victory over the Houston Texans, giving him 46 for the year—two shy of the single-season record Marino set two decades ago.

When asked by the *New York Daily News* how he felt about Manning's pursuit of his record, Dan Marino replied he would not like to see his record broken—"I wouldn't be human if I didn't tell you that"—but he went on to say he was pleased it would be Manning, rather than someone else: "He has a lot of class and he's everything that's right about the NFL and playing the quarterback position." That was high praise from one of the all-time greats.

Manning's big day came on December 26, 2004, against the San Diego Chargers at the RCA Dome. Manning tied Marino's record of 48 touchdowns early in the game, and, with just one minute left to play, he led a drive that pulled the Colts to within two. They then converted a two-point conversion to tie the score and send the game to overtime. Despite breaking the record on the game-tying drive, Manning had asked his teammates not to congratulate him—he wanted to be sure to win the game. In overtime, Mike Vanderjagt kicked the game-winning field goal to give the Colts a 34-31 win. Before the game, Manning had talked to Marino, who was a studio analyst for CBS. Manning recounted how much the record meant to him: "I was getting all emotional talking to him [Marino], I can't believe it," a choked-up Manning said. "Dan, besides my father, was always my favorite player growing up after my dad retired. I would have been content if I would have stayed tied. I would have shared that record." Further questioned by the *New York Daily News* as to how he felt about this day, in which he had thrown for 383 yards, Manning replied, "I think Johnny Unitas [who died in 2002] would have been proud."

Very likely so. Manning ended the season with 49 touchdown passes, 4,557 yards passing, and a 67.6 percent

In the Colts' 34-31 overtime win over the San Diego Chargers on December 26, 2004, Peyton Manning broke Dan Marino's 20-year-old record for touchdown passes in a season. The Colts' signal caller hit wide receiver Brandon Stokley on a 21-yard post pattern with just 56 seconds left in regulation to break Marino's record. Here, fans celebrate with a homemade 49 sign, recognizing Manning's outstanding accomplishment.

**pass completion** rate. In addition, he broke Steve Young's 10-year-old record for the highest passer rating in a season (112.8) when he posted a rating of 121.1. This was, quite possibly, the best single-season performance by any quarterback in NFL history.

## THE PLAYOFFS

Indianapolis went 12–4 in 2004, closing out the season with a 33-14 loss at Denver, in which Coach Dungy rested most of his starters, including Manning. On the other hand, the Broncos had to win the game to get into the playoffs, and they also wanted revenge against the team that had knocked them out of the playoffs the year before. The AFC had become so competitive that the Colts actually entered the playoffs only as a **wild-card** team, with their first opponent being the Broncos. This time the tables were turned, as Manning and the Colts dismantled the Broncos, 49-24. Manning acted like a surgeon, as he picked apart the Denver defense, completing 27 of 33 passes for 458 yards and four touchdowns. In addition to Manning's franchise records for completions and passing yards, the Colts also set franchise playoff records for most points (49) and most first downs (27). At the end of the day, Indianapolis looked like a good bet to reach the Super Bowl. But there was one more hurdle that stood in their way: the New England Patriots.

## HIGHEST PASSER RATING (SEASON) IN NFL HISTORY

| NUMBER | PLAYER |
| --- | --- |
| 121.1 | Peyton Manning, Indianapolis Colts, 2004 |
| 117.2 | Tom Brady, New England Patriots, 2007 |
| 112.8 | Steve Young, San Francisco 49ers, 1994 |

Even now, with a bit of hindsight, no one quite knows what Bill Belichick did to inspire his players against the Colts. Was it another set of Super Bowl rings? Was it a taunt about the relative strength of the defensive units of both teams? No one knows for certain, but Tom Brady and the Patriots came out firing. Michael Silver of *Sports Illustrated* described the stellar play of the Patriots' defense in the two-word title of his article: "Pat Answer."

> Linebacker Tedy Bruschi stood out with a pair of fumble recoveries, taking the ball away from Indianapolis running back Dominic Rhodes while making a **tackle** in the second quarter, then pouncing on a ball that [Rodney] Harrison pried from wideout Reggie Wayne with 6:58 left. But *everyone* on the New England defense played like a star.

New England won, 20-3, in one of the most one-sided of the many games played between the two teams. For Tom Brady and the Patriots, it was the next-to-last step on the way to the Super Bowl, where they beat the Philadelphia Eagles, 24-21. For Manning and the Colts, it was another disappointment. Although he completed 27 of 42 passes for 238 yards in wintry conditions, the Colts could not find the end zone, and Manning dropped to 0–7 all time at New England. Once again, the Colts were confronted with one long offseason in which they would have to come up with answers to the many questions that surrounded their team.

## THE 2005 SEASON

In 2005, Indianapolis started off well and just kept getting better. The Colts beat Baltimore, 24-7; Jacksonville, 10-3; and Cleveland, 13-6. Fans could already see a significant difference in the team's play; the Colts were winning the type of games they had lost in the past. Most of the credit went to Tony

Dungy's improved defense, because Manning was not putting up the overwhelming numbers he had posted a year earlier. That did not seem to matter; like all the rest of the Colts, he was focused on winning a world championship.

In Week 4, the Colts beat Tennessee, 31-10, as Manning completed 20 of 27 passes for 264 yards and four touchdowns. The following week, Indianapolis beat San Francisco, 28-3, then made a Monday Night Football appearance against the St. Louis Rams, winning a wild shootout, 45-28. Having won their first six games was a new kind of thrill, but as the victories continued to mount, the Colts were burdened with trying to break another record. The 1972 Miami Dolphins finished 14–0 during the regular season on their way to a win in Super Bowl VII. Could the Colts start the season 14–0 and match their record? Some team members and even Coach Dungy felt the pressure as they closed in on the record.

The biggest test came on November 7, when the Colts met the Patriots in a heralded Monday Night Football game at New England. Newspapers and magazines made much of the matchup, with most of them calling for "Tom Terrific" Brady to extend his winning ways over the Colts. Although Manning had never beaten the Patriots in New England, he played well this time around, completing 28 of 37 passes for 321 yards and three touchdowns in an easy 40-21 win. He and his team had finally solved at least some of the Patriots' defensive schemes.

New England was without some of its key players that night, but it was really Manning's moment to shine. Even though Brady had a good night on paper—265 yards passing and three touchdowns—the Colts outgained the Patriots 453 to 288 yards. A Boston journalist described the postgame scene:

> Outside the Indianapolis locker room, Peyton Manning talked for a long time about what an important win this was for the Colts, who were now 8–0 on the season. Previously, in this stadium, Manning had stood still

for long disquisitions about how Bill Belichick and the Patriots had caused him to flounder and fail at the biggest moments possible. This was his first win against a Tom Brady-led New England team in six tries and, all in all, Manning handled it graciously.

From there it was on to Houston, where the Colts prevailed, 31-17. Then, after a 45-37 win at Cincinnati, where Manning threw for 365 yards, Indianapolis prepared for another appearance on Monday Night Football, the third for the Colts that season. This time they beat the Pittsburgh Steelers, 26-7, extending their winning streak to start the season to 11 games.

## MANNING TO HARRISON

Just as there had been comparisons between Peyton Manning and Johnny Unitas, analogies were also made between the quarterback-receiver combination of Peyton Manning and Marvin Harrison and Johnny Unitas and Raymond Berry. Born in Philadelphia in 1972, Harrison lost his father to a congenital disease when he was two years old. His mother worked two jobs while raising Marvin and two siblings, and by the time he went to Syracuse University on a football scholarship, Marvin knew the importance of having a solid work ethic and the efforts needed to survive (much of his youth was spent living in dangerous neighborhoods). Following his career at Syracuse, he was selected nineteenth overall by the Indianapolis Colts in the first round of the 1996 NFL draft.

Harrison did well even before Manning arrived in 1998, but once Manning came to town the two became a potent combination. Harrison caught 115 passes for 1,663 yards in

There were two more wins—over the Tennessee Titans, 35-3, and the Jacksonville Jaguars, 26-18—before their undefeated string was snapped at 13 by the San Diego Chargers, 26-17.

Then, just five days later, tragedy struck the team, when, on December 23, 2005, Tony Dungy's 18-year-old son, James, was found dead, the apparent victim of suicide. If Peyton Manning was the team leader and inspiration, Tony Dungy had, during the past four seasons, become its soul. Modest, almost quiet on the sidelines, Dungy rarely yelled about anything. He was more like Tom Landry, the legendary coach of the Dallas Cowboys from 1960 to 1988, than John Madden or Bill Parcells, both of whom were known for their outbursts. "The Lord has a plan,"

1999, 102 for 1,413 yards in 2000, 109 for 1,524 yards in 2001, and a staggering 143 for 1,722 yards in 2002. After those fantastic four seasons, his numbers declined somewhat, partly because Manning was also throwing to wideout Reggie Wayne, but the Manning-to-Harrison combination remained the most productive in the NFL. At the end of his first 10 NFL seasons (1996–2005), Harrison had accounted for 670 points scored by his team. In addition, he holds several NFL records, including receptions in a season (143) and most consecutive seasons with 100 or more receptions (4).

Comparisons between Manning-Harrison, Unitas-Berry, and Montana-Rice abound, but by the end of 2006, there was little doubt that Manning and Harrison were the most productive quarterback-receiver tandem in NFL history. The only question was how much longer were they going to stay together.

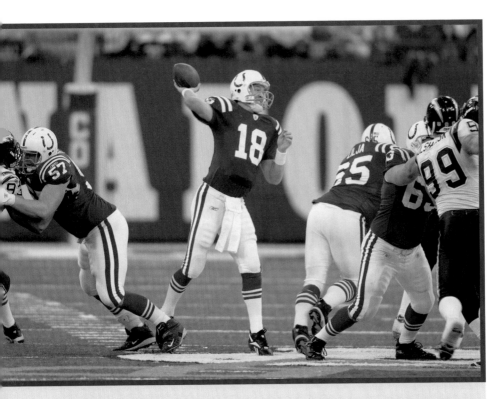

Peyton Manning throws a pass during the Colts' 26-17 loss to the San Diego Chargers on December 18, 2005. The Colts started the season 13–0, and many fans and members of the media thought they might surpass the 1972 Miami Dolphins' perfect record of 14–0. Unfortunately for the Colts, the Chargers had other ideas.

Dungy told ESPN. "We always think the plans are A, B, C and D, and everything is going to be perfect for us and it may not be that way, but it's still his plan. A lot of tremendous things are going to happen, it just may not be the way you see them."

Coach Dungy did not comment much on his son's suicide, but the event clearly affected the Indianapolis Colts. Not only did they grieve for their coach's loss, but they missed his ultra-steady hand at the controls when he missed their game against the Seattle Seahawks on Christmas Eve. The Colts rested most of their starters in preparation for the playoffs and dropped the game to the Seahawks, 28-13. In the final regular-season game,

Coach Dungy returned to the sidelines, and the Colts again rested most of their starters, but this time they defeated the Arizona Cardinals, 17-13, at the RCA Dome.

Despite earning the number-one seed in the playoffs, the Colts were upset at home in the divisional round, falling to the Pittsburgh Steelers, 21-18, on January 15, 2006. Those who had watched the Colts in their first 13 games of the season, including their win over the Steelers on Monday Night Football, wondered if this was the same team. Manning, Coach Dungy, and the entire Colts organization had made a terrific charge during the regular season, but they faltered again at the end.

Manning was still only 29 at the time the Steelers knocked the Colts out of the playoffs, but he was already beginning to hear people say, "Wait 'till next year," a humiliating comparison between his career and that of the Boston Red Sox, who had gone without a World Series championship between 1918 and 2004 (when they finally broke "The Curse" and defeated the St. Louis Cardinals in the World Series). For Manning, next year could not come soon enough.

# Miracle Season

**P**eyton Manning did not believe in miracles or supernatural assistance. Like Coach Tony Dungy, he was a serious believer in hard work and executing the fundamentals of football. Even so, when one examines the 2006 NFL season, one wonders if the Colts had some extra help in carrying off one of the most impressive seasons of all time.

## THE RUN BEGINS

The 2006 season began with the much-heralded matchup between Peyton and his younger brother, Eli, on Monday Night Football. In what was dubbed the "Manning Bowl," the Colts beat the New York Giants, 26-21, in a game that showcased the talents of the Manning brothers. Both quarterbacks performed well, but Peyton and the Colts were a bit better than

Eli and the Giants, taking an important Week 1 win. Then it was back to Indianapolis for the home opener against the Houston Texans.

The five-year-old Texans franchise was 0–9 all time against the Colts, and observers expected the results to be the same on this occasion. Coach Dungy and other Colts coaches called this a potential "trap game," meaning that it was in situations like these (where they were heavily favored) that the Colts had sometimes lost in the past. This time, they performed with alacrity, beating the Texans, 43-24. Manning completed 26 of 38 passes for 400 yards and three touchdowns, but more important, in the first quarter, he connected on his 2,797th career completion, breaking Johnny Unitas's franchise record for completions. Texans quarterback David Carr—who was sacked four times in the game—summed up the Texans' frustration best in *True Blue: The Colts Unforgettable 2006 Championship Season* when he said: "Coming up here [to Indianapolis] is a chore."

A week later, on September 24, the Colts hosted the Jacksonville Jaguars, their chief competition in the AFC South Division. When one looks at the game statistics, it seems impossible to believe that the Jaguars lost: They led in yards rushing (191 to 63), total yards gained (297 to 272), first downs (20 to 14), and **time of possession** (39:24 to 20:36). Yet the Colts prevailed, 21-14. They were steady throughout the game, scoring a touchdown in the second, third, and fourth quarters, while the Jaguars started off fast, with one in the first, and finished well, with one in the fourth. Manning was very workmanlike in completing 14 of 31 passes for 219 yards and a touchdown. He and Coach Dungy were philosophical about the Colts' slow start in which they only had the ball for three series in the first half, for a total of nine plays: "We did keep our composure," said Dungy in *True Blue: The Colts' Unforgettable 2006 Championship Season.*

Peyton Manning gets the ball off right before being hit during the Colts' 43-24 win against the Houston Texans on September 17, 2006. Manning completed 26 of 38 passes for 400 yards and three touchdowns in the win. He also broke Johnny Unitas's franchise record for career completions when he connected on number 2,797 of his career during the first quarter.

"Obviously, you have to move on. At the time, if you spend a lot of time complaining about it, it's going to affect you the next play."

Next it was back to Giants Stadium to face the New York Jets. Manning and the Colts felt confident heading into the game against the 2–1 Jets, but the contest turned out to be closer, tighter, and more difficult than their opening-season game against the Giants in the same stadium.

The Colts got out in front, with a first-quarter touchdown, and they added a second touchdown in the second quarter, but the Jets roared back with two touchdowns in the second quarter to even the score at 14-14 heading into halftime. After a scoreless third quarter, the game seesawed back and forth in the fourth quarter. The Colts took the lead, 17-14, on a 20-yard Martin Gramatica field goal, but the Jets regained the lead, 21-17, with just under eight minutes left to play. The Colts responded with a 12-play, 68-yard drive to pull ahead, 24-21, with 2:40 left in the game. However, on the very next play, Jets kick returner Justin Miller took back the kick 103 yards to seemingly give the Jets control of the game, 28-24. With no timeouts and barely more than two minutes left in the game, Manning led the Colts to the twenty-fourth game-winning touchdown drive of his career, completing 6 of 8 passes on the drive for 60 yards. He then scored from one yard out to cap the drive and give the Colts a 31-28 win.

The Tennessee Titans, a team that had always proven tough in the past but was 0–4 this season, came to Indianapolis for the fifth regular-season game. The Titans stormed ahead with seven points in the first quarter and three in the second to lead 10-0 at the half. But the Colts responded in the second half. Manning threw two touchdown passes to give the Colts a 14-13 win, which illustrated how much tougher and more resilient the 2006 Colts were than the team of years past. This meant that Indianapolis was 5–0 heading into its bye week, during which the players hoped to get some much-needed rest and prepare for the stretch run.

## THE MIDDLE OF THE SEASON

On October 22, the Colts hosted the Washington Redskins at the RCA Dome. Washington had the reputation of being a very physical team, and its players lived up to it in the first half.

Manning took a number of hits in the second quarter, one of them bad enough to knock him out of the game shortly before halftime (though he would not miss a snap). The Colts were forced to call a timeout after the vicious hit. "I don't spend a lot of time thinking or talking about it. Nobody likes to burn a timeout. I'd rather take a delay-of-game penalty sometimes than call a first-or-second-quarter timeout," Manning said in *True Blue: The Colts' Unforgettable 2006 Championship Season*. When newspaper reporters tried to get more information about what injury he might have suffered, Manning simply replied, "You're not going to get much from me on that." He knew that the Colts, like any football team, thrived on momentum, and that it was up to him to lead the team in many ways, which included showing how tough he was. Indianapolis trailed 14-13 at the half, but the Redskins did not know what was about to hit them.

Manning came out blazing in the third quarter, leading three drives that resulted in 20 points. During his torrid third-quarter performance, he completed 7 of 8 passes for 138 yards. All told, he completed 25 of 35 passes for 342 yards and four touchdowns in the Colts' 36-22 win—the team's eighteenth in its last 20 games at the RCA Dome. In addition, he moved into fourth place on the all-time NFL list with his fourteenth four-touchdown game of his career.

The Colts followed the win with a 34-31 victory over the Broncos at Denver, behind a stunning 32 of 39 performance by Manning. The win moved the Colts to 7–0 on the season; the first time an NFL team accomplished that feat in back-to-back seasons since the Green Bay Packers did it from 1929 to 1931. But all eyes were on the matchup that followed, pitting Manning and the Colts against Tom Brady and the Patriots in New England. The eighth regular-season game was played at Foxborough on a Sunday night, with 68,000 fans at Gillette Stadium and millions more watching on television.

There was no doubting the importance of the game. New England had beaten Indianapolis so many times during

Manning's career that some Patriots fans thought the matter was a foregone conclusion. But there was no snow this time, no blinding whiteouts, just a sharply cold night in the darkness of New England.

Manning and the Colts struck first. They scored a touchdown on their first possession of the game and scored on two more possessions to take a 17-14 lead into the half. Although Brady and the Patriots needed to answer with touchdowns, all they could manage were a pair of second-half field goals. The much-maligned Colts' defense, which was last in the NFL against the run heading into the game, began to show some signs of life by forcing five turnovers. The Patriots usually prevailed in low-scoring games that featured field goals, but their longtime kicker Adam Vinatieri was now playing for the Colts, and, despite missing two field goals, he did manage to boot two through the uprights. In the end, Manning outplayed Tom Brady for the second time in a row, completing 20 of 36 passes for 326 yards, two touchdowns, and just one interception in the Colts' 27-20 win. Manning relished the moment in *True Blue: The Colts' Unforgettable 2006 Championship Season*:

> It was a great win, a great team win. To beat these guys, especially here, that's got to be as a team. Everybody has to contribute—all phases of it.

## A TOUGH END TO THE REGULAR SEASON

Suddenly, the Colts were the team to watch and the team to beat. With the win in Foxborough, they improved their record to 8–0 and had won an amazing 30 of their last 33 regular-season contests. They made it 9–0 a week later, with a 17-16 win over Buffalo, but that was the end of their spectacular run to start the season. Despite losing three out of their next four games, including setbacks to Dallas, 21-14; Tennessee, 20-17; and Jacksonville, 44-17, the Colts had made history by becoming the first team in the NFL ever to start 9–0 in consecutive seasons. The Colts recovered in Week 15 to down the Cincinnati Bengals, 34-16, behind four touchdown passes from Manning, but they again lost to another AFC South Division opponent the following week; this time to the Houston Texans, 27-24. (It was the first time the Texans had ever beaten Indianapolis.) Even though they won their last regular-season game against the Dolphins, 27-22, the Colts were seemingly stumbling into the playoffs with a 12–4 record. Their superb 9–0 start was a distant memory, and though they won the AFC South Division, they would have to play during the wild-card round of the playoffs. But there was a bigger problem that was once again rearing its head: The Colts were unable to stop the run in their final few games. In their losses to Tennessee, Jacksonville, and Houston, they gave up an average of 262 yards per game on the ground, including a staggering 375 in the loss to Jacksonville (the second-highest total since the NFL/AFL merger in 1970). Yes, their record was good enough to give them a home game in the wild-card round of the playoffs, but their late-season swoon dropped them to the third overall seed in the AFC. How would the Colts and the NFL's worst run defense respond against a team with one of the most potent running attacks in the NFL—the Kansas City Chiefs?

## THE WILD-CARD ROUND

Indianapolis had a winning record against Kansas City, but the two teams had a long tradition of tough battles, with one or the other usually prevailing in the last few minutes of the game. This time, Manning and the Colts slammed the door on the Chiefs behind a surprisingly stingy defense.

Coach Dungy closed practice to reporters in the week leading up to the playoff game; he did not want the Chiefs to see how he planned to revamp the Colts' defensive unit. It was a wise decision, because the Colts' offense struggled, especially in the early going. Despite Indianapolis taking a 9-0 halftime lead on the strength of three Adam Vinatieri field goals and the solid play of the Colts' defense, Manning threw two first-half interceptions. What was different about a defense that gave up just 24 yards rushing in the first half? Coach Dungy later claimed, "We really didn't change anything," but that seemed disingenuous. How had the Colts' defense, so poor in the second half of the regular season, gotten so much better against the Chiefs? No one was really going to answer that question, least of all the coach who had made it happen.

The Chiefs finally got on the scoreboard with just 14 seconds left in the third quarter, but it was too little too late. The Colts took control of the game when a fourth-quarter touchdown pass from Manning to Reggie Wayne gave them a 23-8 lead, which they held onto for the final 10 minutes of the game. The Colts' performance was impressive: They gained 435 total yards (to 126 for the Chiefs) and had 28 first downs (compared to just seven for Kansas City). In addition, rookie tailback Joseph Addai, who replaced longtime Colt Edgerrin James in the backfield in 2006, showed his worth to the team, running for 122 yards on the day. But the most important stat may have been 0–11. That was the Colts' all-time record when Manning threw three or more interceptions in a game. Despite tossing three in this game, the Colts easily beat the Chiefs. Was this an omen that it was finally the Colts' year?

There was little rest for the weary, as Indianapolis had to prepare to meet the Baltimore Ravens on January 13. This game would be played in Baltimore, where the Ravens had a 42–14 home record since 2000, the best in the NFL.

## AFC DIVISIONAL GAME

The AFC South Division champions, the Colts, went to Baltimore to play the AFC North Division champions, the Ravens, for the right to play in the AFC Championship Game. Not only were the two teams well matched physically and statistically, but Baltimore fans would have liked nothing more than for their team to knock out their former team from the playoffs.

Although it had been more than 20 years since Robert Irsay moved the Colts to Indianapolis, Baltimore fans had long memories. Colts-Ravens games were usually very competitive, and given the fact that this was the first time the two teams met in the playoffs, the game was even bigger.

Manning and the Colts took the ball 49 yards on their first possession, and Adam Vinatieri capped the drive with a field goal. Although the Colts and Ravens did not know it at the time, this play established the pattern for a game in which neither side would score a single touchdown. The Colts headed into halftime with a 9-3 lead behind three field goals from Vinatieri, whom the Colts had signed during the offseason for his clutch kicking. Thanks to each team's stout defense, neither quarterback lit up the scoreboard in the first half: Manning threw for just 77 yards, while the Ravens' Steve McNair threw for just 60 yards. McNair managed to do a little better in the second half, but the Ravens' offense could never get closer than the Colts' 33-yard line, and Baltimore could only manage a 51-yard field goal in the final 30 minutes. On the ground, the Ravens managed just 17 yards in the second half, thanks to the Colts' revitalized defense. The Colts added another field goal in each of the final two quarters to earn a hard-fought 15-6 win. The win was not pretty, but even before the game, Manning had grown tired of the press's repeated questions about the Colts' lack of offensive production during the playoffs. He said in *True Blue: The Colts' Unforgettable 2006 Championship Season*:

> A lot of people say, "Throw the statistics out the window in the playoffs and just get a win." But it's like we're the exception. . . . You do whatever you can to try to make a couple of big third-down conversions, you take your field goals where you can.

The Colts had done just that, kicking a total of five field goals, all from the right foot of Adam Vinatieri. The victory over Baltimore meant that the Colts would now play for the AFC Championship, and, because of New England's spectacular 24-21 come-from-behind victory over the San Diego Chargers, the game would be played in the RCA Dome. It would be the first time Indianapolis had hosted an AFC Championship Game, and the team was ready to get the monkey off its back.

## AFC CHAMPIONS

The New England Patriots came to Indianapolis secure in the knowledge that they had won their last five AFC Championship games, but all of those wins had come outside. This time, the Patriots had to play in the comfortable confines of the RCA Dome, where Manning and the Colts did not have to worry about the elements. And despite boasting a winning record in head-to-head matchups against Manning and the Colts, the Patriots had lost the last two contests, both of which were in New England. Indianapolis also had won nine straight games in the RCA Dome, so history seemed to favor the Colts.

Most commentators believed that Manning was a better all-around quarterback than Tom Brady, but that the latter was still the best when it came to winning in the clutch. Most observers agreed this would be a close, hard-fought game.

From the beginning of the game, Manning came out throwing. He completed 13 of 24 passes for 124 yards in the first half, but he was intercepted once, and the Patriots' defensive **secondary** played superbly, batting away a number of Manning's passes. Not only did New England's defense frustrate the Colts, but the Patriots' offense went on the attack. New England scored its first touchdown on an eight-play, 75-yard drive that culminated in a bit of luck. After driving to the Colts' 4-yard line, Brady fumbled the ball, but it was eventually recovered by Patriots offensive **guard** Logan Mankins in the end zone for a touchdown. The Colts responded with a 42-

yard Adam Vinatieri field goal, but the Patriots came right back to take a 14-3 lead on a seven-yard touchdown run by tailback Corey Dillon. Then, on the ensuing drive, Manning was intercepted by Patriots cornerback Asante Samuel, who returned it 39 yards for a touchdown and a commanding 21-3 lead with 9:25 left in the first half. At this point, the Colts had to feel that they were snakebit, as the majority of the 57,433 fans in attendance sat silently in disbelief. It looked as if New England's mastery would continue.

When the teams went to their respective locker rooms, the Colts were behind, 21-6. The deficit did not bother the Colts as much as the memory of the many losses to New England in the past. Even Manning was down. But the moment belonged to Coach Dungy, who walked quietly around the locker room before looking Manning in the eyes and saying, "I'm telling you, this is our game."

The statement seemed ridiculous. Here the Colts were, down by 15 points to their nemesis, and Coach Dungy was speaking of victory? But the coach had been watching the game closely, and he believed the New England defense was about to wear down. The Patriots' defensive players had been fantastic in the first half, but the pressure of continually defending Manning's long bombs would eventually catch up to them. In a *Sports Illustrated* article, Manning later remembered:

> Tony is one calm customer, no matter what the circumstances, and he has a way of making you believe. We're stressed out, and he's parading back and forth telling us we're going to win. That rubs off on the younger players, even the older players. It made a difference.

Coach Dungy knew best. The Colts came out swinging in the third quarter. Manning led them on a 14-play, 76-yard drive that ended with a quick sneak into the end zone by the quarterback himself. That made the score 21-13. The Patriots then went three-and-out, and they were forced to punt the ball back to the Colts. This time, Manning led them on a shorter, six-play drive, but it still culminated in a touchdown and pulled the Colts to within two points. After Marvin Harrison converted a two-point conversion, the game was tied at 21-21.

How many times, commentators asked, had the Patriots and Colts been in this position, with the score tied in the second half? Far too often.

But then Tom Brady showed again why he is one of the best in the business. After an 80-yard kickoff return by Ellis Hobbs set the Patriots up at the Colts' 21-yard line, Brady completed a six-yard touchdown pass to wide receiver Jabar Gaffney to give the Patriots a 28-21 lead. However, Manning and the Colts came right back, tying the game after **center** Jeff Saturday recovered a Dominic Rhodes fumble in the end zone much like the Patriots' Logan Mankins had done earlier in the game. After each team could do nothing on their next possession, New England's Stephen Gostkowski kicked a field goal with 7:45 left to put the Patriots up, 31-28. But Adam Vinatieri answered with a 36-yard field goal, before Gostkowski came right back to boot a 43-yard field goal with less than four minutes left in the game. Again, the two teams traded possessions, before Manning trotted onto the field with just 2:17 to play. Starting at his own 20-yard line, he took the Colts right down the field, highlighted by two Reggie Wayne catches and a 32-yard pass to tight end Bryan Fletcher. The drive was capped off by a three-yard touchdown run by Joseph Addai, which gave the Colts a 38-34 lead with just 1:02 left in the game.

After leading the drive, Manning sat on the sidelines, agitation evident in his body language. As Tom Brady came out onto the field, for one last attempt to win the game, Manning buried his face in a towel: He could not bear to think that the Patriots might deny the Colts yet again.

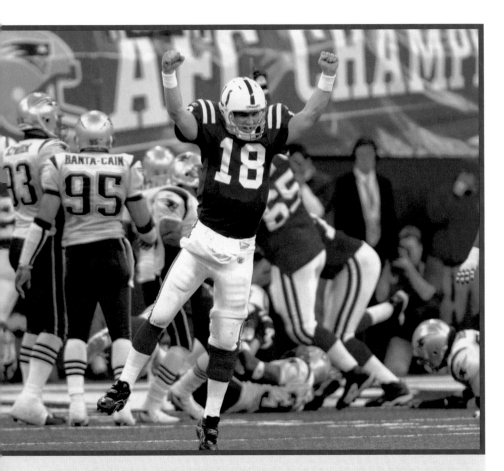

Peyton Manning celebrates after Indianapolis running back Joseph Addai scores on a three-yard touchdown run in the fourth quarter that provided the winning margin in the Colts' 38-34 victory over the New England Patriots. The win not only was the Colts' third straight over the Patriots, but it also propelled Indianapolis to the Super Bowl.

Even the great ones falter sometimes, and with 24 seconds left on the clock, Brady threw a pass that was intercepted by Colts cornerback Marlin Jackson. They had done it! The Colts had defeated their nemesis and were on their way to play in their first Super Bowl (and the franchise's first since 1970)! Much of the credit had to be given to Manning, who had an outstanding game, completing 27 of 47 passes for 349 yards and a touchdown.

## RACE THROUGH THE RAIN

The Colts arrived in Miami a week before Super Bowl XLI. Manning made himself rather unpopular with some of his teammates by suggesting they adopt a no visitation rule during those seven days: no friends, no family, no spouses. His idea was adopted by Coach Dungy, and the Colts got down to business throughout the last week of January 2007, preparing for the biggest game of their lives.

Their opponent was the Chicago Bears, a team that had won many laurels over the years, but whose last Super Bowl appearance had been in January 1986. If the Chicago Bears had history and tradition on their side, then the Indianapolis Colts had youth and raw hunger on theirs: Despite Manning's brilliance and the stellar performance of many other Colts players, neither he nor they had ever reached a Super Bowl while playing for Indianapolis.

The same could not be said about Tony Dungy. As a Pittsburgh Steeler, he had played in Super Bowl XIII, and, if he was lucky enough to win this one, he would be one of only three men ever to win a Super Bowl as a player and then as a coach. For Dungy, the week leading up to the Super Bowl was especially meaningful, for the rival team was coached by Lovie Smith (also an African American), who had been one of Dungy's assistant coaches while he was the head coach at Tampa Bay. The two men were good friends, and this was the first time in the history of the Super Bowl that two black head coaches would square off.

The Bears won the toss, and the Colts kicked off. As Colts players streaked down the field to cover the kick, one lone Chicago Bear ran right past them—in the other direction. Chicago rookie Devin Hester received the kick on his own 8-yard line and ran it all the way back for a 92-yard game-opening touchdown (the only time in Super Bowl history that an opening kick was returned in such dramatic fashion). The Indianapolis Colts were in a 7-0 hole, just seconds into the game.

At almost the same time, a light rain began to fall, creating yet another Super Bowl "first"—the first to be played in rainy conditions. All things being equal, this was considered a real plus for the Chicago Bears, who were more accustomed to inclement weather. The Bears had a good first quarter, while Manning struggled. Whether he threw deep or short seemed to make little difference; his timing was off and the whole team seemed to feel the ill effects. Unfortunately, some commentators did not think Manning could turn it around and were beginning to pen those immortal words: "Can't win the Big One." But, as *Sports Illustrated* put it:

## THE HALFTIME SHOW

When the first Super Bowl was played at the Los Angeles Coliseum in 1967, there was no fanfare and almost a third of the seats were empty. That was certainly not the case in 2007.

During the past four decades, the Super Bowl has become an unofficial national holiday, with more people watching the event on television than any other show. This made television executives hungry for advertising dollars, and, over the years, it transformed the Super Bowl into the biggest sporting event in the United States.

The first truly "big" television advertisement aired in 1984, the year Apple unveiled its new Macintosh computer at the expense of IBM. During the 23 years since, Super Bowl ads have become even bigger and bolder, and so has the halftime show. In 2004, the halftime show created quite a controversy because of a song-and-dance act that had pop singer Justin Timberlake

Manning settled the Colts' nerves with 6:58 left in the first quarter. On third-and-10 from the Indy 47 he called for 66 D X-Pump, a play [offensive coordinator Tom] Moore installed for the Super Bowl that called for [Reggie] Wayne, lined up to the left side, to run an in-and-go route designed to exploit Chicago's Cover Two zone scheme.

The plan worked, and Indianapolis cut the lead to 7-6, after Adam Vinatieri missed the extra point. Rather than allow Hester to hurt them again, the Colts kicked the ball short. Bears tight

appear to expose Janet Jackson's breast. Calls had been issued for a "cleaner" halftime show, and the sponsors of Super Bowl XLI were happy to oblige.

Prince, who changed his name back from "The Artist formerly known as Prince," was the main act. His most famous songs, including "Purple Rain" and "Little Red Corvette," had been hits during the 1980s, and he performed them with all his old flair. Still, it seemed a little bizarre to give top billing to an artist whose major success had come 20 years earlier. It was a bit like having the Beatles perform at the 1980 Super Bowl. In one final bit of irony, Prince's biggest single, released in 1983, had been "1999," which included the lyrics "Tonight I'm gonna party like it's 1999." Well, the millennium had come and gone, but Prince was still there, and for Bears fans, they wanted to party like it was 1986—the last time Chicago had won the Super Bowl.

Peyton Manning and Tony Dungy celebrate after the Colts' 29-17 victory in Super Bowl XLI at Miami's Dolphin Stadium on February 4, 2007. Manning was named MVP of the game after completing 25 of 38 passes for 247 yards and a touchdown in the win.

end Gabe Reid then fumbled the ball, which the Colts recovered. Manning came out for another offensive drive, but he fumbled the ball on a handoff to running back Joseph Addai. Before the spectators could gather their breath, the Bears once again had the ball. (The wet weather contributed to a total of eight turnovers on the day, five blunders by Chicago and three by Indianapolis.)

Given their best chance of the game, the Bears got into scoring position on a 52-yard run by tailback Thomas Jones.

Three plays later, Bears quarterback Rex Grossman hit receiver Muhsin Muhammad for a four-yard touchdown pass. Chicago now led 14-6, heading into the second quarter, but the momentum was about to swing in a major way.

In the second quarter, the Colts cut the Bears lead to 14-9 on the strength of an Adam Vinatieri 29-yard field goal. They then took the lead for good when tailback Dominic Rhodes ran in from one yard out to give the Colts a 16-14 lead heading into halftime. In the locker room there was confidence, even jubilation, for the Colts felt certain they could contain Grossman. That proved true enough in the third and fourth quarters, but the Indianapolis defense did not have to work that hard, for the Colts' offense held possession of the ball throughout most of the third quarter. During that quarter, Vinatieri kicked two field goals. Then the Colts finished off the Bears with a 56-yard interception return for a touchdown by cornerback Kelvin Hayden, giving Indianapolis a 29-17 win. Manning was named MVP of the game after he completed 25 of 38 passes for 247 yards and a touchdown.

To say that Peyton Manning was elated is an understatement. To say that Tony Dungy was thrilled does not come nearly close to describing his mind-set. No, to say the Colts had exorcised their demons was closer to the mark. Team president Bill Polian said it best in *True Blue: The Colts' Unforgettable 2006 Championship Season*:

> We buried virtually everything tonight. We're built to play in a dome indoors. We can't play in bad weather. We can't play on grass. We can't stop the run. We can't play against people who are bigger and tougher than we are. We're too small. Peyton Manning can't win the big one. Tony Dungy can't win the big one.

The Colts had arrived; they had finally won that elusive Super Bowl. And Peyton Manning had proved his critics wrong. He was no quitter; he was a fighter.

# On Top
# of the World

**"T**o the victor belong the spoils," is an old expression, one originally meant in a political sense, but it also aptly describes whatever team wins the Super Bowl. Peyton Manning and the Colts reveled in the attention they received after their win over the Bears in Super Bowl XLI.

Manning had been the hottest NFL commodity in advertising for the two years since he had broken Dan Marino's single-season touchdown record, but his popularity soared to new heights after winning the big game. Every major company wanted Manning to endorse their product, and he was able to pick and choose from many offers.

Now that the burden of being unable to win the championship was removed, Manning seemed to enjoy life more. He had a happy marriage; his home life was settled and peaceful;

Peyton Manning and the Indianapolis Colts present President George W. Bush with a jersey during their trip to the White House on April 23, 2007. For Manning, the trip was part of a whirlwind tour after the Super Bowl. In addition to his visit to Washington, D.C., Manning appeared on the *Late Show with David Letterman* and *Saturday Night Live* and was the official starter for the Indianapolis 500.

but there was also a newfound enthusiasm about the way he conducted himself in public. President George W. Bush (who hosted Manning and the Colts at the White House on April 23, 2007) remarked that Manning was a man more sought after by the television networks than the president himself. Perhaps the biggest surprise, however, was Manning's appearance on the popular television show *Saturday Night Live*, then in its thirty-third year, on March 25, 2007.

### SATURDAY NIGHT LIVE

Those who expected Manning to have a difficult time on television did not know that he had majored in speech communication at the University of Tennessee; nor did they know that his consuming passion to be the best helped him succeed at whatever he did. Although no press release announced the manner of Manning's preparation for *Saturday Night Live*, one can be confident he did prepare. He began the show:

> Thank you! Thank you very much! It's such an honor and a thrill to be hosting *Saturday Night Live*. It's been a fun year for me, as I've accomplished two lifelong goals: 1) I appeared in over *half* of America's television commercials, and uh, my team, the Colts, won the Super Bowl.

Archie, Olivia, and Eli Manning were all there to see Peyton in his moment of glory. They were introduced to the audience while Peyton rambled on, cracking jokes at their expense. For instance, he said the following about his mother:

> She didn't make it to the NFL—uh—she didn't really have what it took. She got cut by the Dolphins, she tried in Canada for a bit, uh—she's a real disappointment to all of us, but she's still a great lady and we love her.

Manning also poked fun at himself. Recently, he said, he had visited a longtime friend in Boston who had posed a question to him: What do Tom Brady and the circus have in common? The answer, sure enough, was that they both had two more rings than Manning!

Hosting the show with pop singer Carrie Underwood, Manning engaged in some self parody in which he and Underwood (using different names) acted as if they were an average guy and girl picking winners and losers in the NBA (National Basketball Association). When Underwood mentioned that a team was favored, but that it might "pull" a Peyton Manning, Peyton asked what that meant. "Oh you know," she replied, "having all the statistics and numbers, but losing when it counts."

A year earlier, that joke may have hit a little too close to home for Manning, but with a Super Bowl victory behind him, he could afford to be magnanimous and to look like an idiot on television. Reminding his viewers that he had never suffered from a lack of motivation, Manning vowed to return to the field with a vengeance that fall, suggesting he would beat the New England Patriots and anyone else who got in his way.

It goes without saying that Manning has earned his success and fame. He has certainly become one of the most recognizable faces in the United States—right up there with the president and Hollywood stars. But if one were able to get close to Manning (and that has become increasingly difficult over the years), one generally gets the impression that here was a celebrity who was not overcome by his fame; that he was still the unpretentious boy raised by Archie and Olivia Manning.

## COMMUNITY SERVICE

This unpretentious boy has become a man who enjoys using his fame and fortune to give back to the community. Manning is involved in several philanthropic causes, but he devotes the majority of his time to the PeyBack Foundation, which he established in 1999 to "promote the future success of disadvantaged youth by helping programs that provide the necessary leadership and growth opportunities for youth at risk." The foundation focuses on assisting long-standing community-based programs and providing rudimentary leadership and growth opportunities for children. It works with organizations in Indiana, Tennessee, and Louisiana. Since its inception, the foundation has donated more than $1.3 million, including more than $115,000 in 2006 to aid Hurricane Katrina relief in New Orleans. The foundation's largest fund-raising event is the PeyBack Bowl, which, since

2003, has raised more than $850,000 for underprivileged children in Indianapolis. Such celebrities as NBC sports anchor Bob Costas, former Baltimore Orioles Hall of Fame shortstop Cal Ripken Jr., and NASCAR great Tony Stewart have participated in the event.

In addition to this event, the PeyBack Foundation is involved in several other community service projects, including the PeyBack Classic and the Peyton's Pals program. Started in 2000, the PeyBack Classic gives four inner-city Indianapolis high school football teams the opportunity to play in the RCA Dome, with all proceeds donated to each school's athletic department. The Peyton's Pals program was established in 2003 and gives 20 inner-city middle-school students the opportunity to experience a series of educational, cultural, and community service activities throughout the course of a year. In the past, such events have included an excursion to see the play the *Lion King*, an overnight trip to Kings Island amusement park in Cincinnati, tickets to Colts games, and the opportunity to do volunteer work with the Indiana chapter of the Special Olympics.

Manning's work in the community has been recognized and appreciated by many people—from New Orleans to Indianapolis—but perhaps the most important honor he received for his off-the-field work was given to him in February 2006, when he was named the winner of the Walter Payton NFL Man of the Year Award. Presented annually to an NFL player who shows exemplary work in the community and on the field, the award is named after NFL Hall of Fame running back Walter Payton, who tragically died in 1999 as the result of complications from a rare liver disease called primary sclerosing cholangitis. Upon accepting the award, Manning said: "This award is one I'll cherish forever in part for the man it's named after and in part because it represents community service. With the great advantages of being an NFL quarterback comes great responsibility to make a difference in the community."

On February 3, 2006, Peyton Manning was given the Walter Payton NFL Man of the Year Award, which is presented annually to an NFL player for his exemplary volunteer and charity work and for his play on the field. Manning is pictured here with Connie Payton, the wife of deceased NFL Hall of Fame running back Walter Payton, whom the award is named for, and Gene Upshaw, president of the NFL Players Association.

## COMPARING MANNING TO NFL GREATS

With his stellar play on the football field, Peyton Manning will inevitably be compared with other football greats, both of his own time and those of the past. While every big football fan will have his or her own answers to the following questions, we will pose them and present some possible answers.

- Is Manning the "best" player of his time?
- How does he compare to past greats such as John Elway, Dan Marino, and Johnny Unitas?

# WALTER PAYTON NFL MAN OF THE YEAR AWARD WINNERS

| YEAR | PLAYER | POSITION | TEAM |
|------|--------|----------|------|
| 2006 | Drew Brees/ | Quarterback | New Orleans Saints |
|      | LaDainian Tomlinson | Running back | San Diego Chargers |
| 2005 | **Peyton Manning** | **Quarterback** | **Indianapolis Colts** |
| 2004 | Warrick Dunn | Running back | Altanta Falcons |
| 2003 | Will Shields | Offensive guard | Kansas City Chiefs |
| 2002 | Troy Vincent | Cornerback | Philadelphia Eagles |
| 2001 | Jerome Bettis | Running back | Pittsburgh Steelers |
| 2000 | Derrick Brooks/ | Linebacker | Tampa Bay Buccaneers |
|      | Jim Flanigan | Defensive tackle | Chicago Bears |
| 1999 | Cris Carter | Wide receiver | Minnesota Vikings |
| 1998 | Dan Marino | Quarterback | Miami Dolphins |
| 1997 | Troy Aikman | Quarterback | Dallas Cowboys |
| 1996 | Darrell Green | Cornerback | Washington Redskins |
| 1995 | Boomer Esiason | Quarterback | New York Jets |
| 1994 | Junior Seau | Linebacker | San Diego Chargers |
| 1993 | Derrick Thomas | Linebacker | Kansas City Chiefs |
| 1992 | John Elway | Quarterback | Denver Broncos |
| 1991 | Anthony Munoz | Offensive tackle | Cincinnati Bengals |
| 1990 | Mike Singletary | Linebacker | Chicago Bears |
| 1989 | Warren Moon | Quarterback | Houston Oilers |
| 1988 | Steve Largent | Wide receiver | Seattle Seahawks |
| 1987 | Dave Duerson | Safety | Chicago Bears |
| 1986 | Reggie Williams | Linebacker | Cincinnati Bengals |
| 1985 | Dwight Stephenson | Center | Miami Dolphins |

Manning is undeniably the best quarterback of his time. His statistics simply speak for themselves: the most seasons with 4,000 or more yards passing (8), consecutive seasons with 25 or more touchdown passes (10), and highest passer rating in a season (121.1), and the second-most touchdown passes in a season (49), just to name a few. He has only two contemporaries who can be compared to him: Tom Brady of New England and Brett Favre of Green Bay.

Critics would be quick to point out that it is unfair to compare Manning with Favre, because the latter's career began in 1991. But there is one major comparison that can be drawn: durability. Favre holds the all-time record for consecutive starts with his team and at the quarterback position in NFL history. Beginning in 1992, he has started every single game for Green Bay (the number had reached 253 through the 2007 season).

Manning actually has a chance to catch Favre, whose career is winding down. But it would take Manning another six years to even Favre's mark, and many people wonder if the Colts quarterback can continue to enjoy such an injury-free career. But in terms of sheer toughness, the two were almost exactly even. Favre has not missed a single start in 16 seasons, and Manning has missed one (exactly one!) snap due to injury in his 10 years with the Colts—that one had been because of a broken jaw! In addition, Favre set several NFL career records during the 2007 season, including most wins by a quarterback, most passing yards, and most touchdown passes. However, all of these records are well within Manning's reach, if he plays a half-dozen more years and stays healthy. Then there is the inevitable comparison with Tom Brady.

## MOST TOUCHDOWN PASSES IN A SEASON

| NUMBER | PLAYER |
|---|---|
| 50 | Tom Brady, New England Patriots, 2007 |
| 49 | Peyton Manning, Indianapolis Colts, 2004 |
| 48 | Dan Marino, Miami Dolphins, 1984 |

Manning's statistics—his overall touchdown numbers and passing percentages especially—are far better than Brady's, but Brady has proven to be a clutch player whose most impressive statistic is his number of big-game wins. During the 2006 season, it seemed that Manning and the Colts had finally gained the upper hand on Brady and the Patriots, but both quarterbacks figure to be in the league for at least a few more years, so the rivalry should continue. Perhaps one can put it this way: There were moments in the 2006 season and in the playoffs when Brady was absolutely fantastic, when he was a more accurate passer than Manning, but during the entire season, Manning's performance was generally better than Brady's. The two were certainly worthy opponents, and their inspired matchups made the NFL more exciting.

It is difficult to compare Manning with Dan Marino and John Elway (both of whom retired in the late 1990s). The Indianapolis Colts of 1998 through 2007 were different from the Denver Broncos and the Miami Dolphins. At his best, Dan Marino was as good a passer as anyone has ever been in NFL history (though, sadly, he never won a Super Bowl), and John Elway was the best come-from-behind quarterback in NFL history. (During his career, he led the Broncos to 47 wins when they faced a fourth-quarter deficit.) As with Favre, if Manning plays for another five or six years, then his statistics will surely surpass Marino's and Elway's.

And what of Johnny Unitas, the man most identified with the Baltimore Colts? Unitas occupies a nearly unique position in football history. He was a 10-time Pro Bowl player and three-time NFL MVP. In comparison, Manning is an eight-time Pro Bowl player and has won the NFL MVP Award twice. In this day and age when quarterbacks throw the ball a good deal more than during the 1950s and 1960s, Manning's career statistics will surely outshine Unitas's. However, many people consider Unitas the greatest player of all time, and his record of 47 consecutive games with a touchdown pass may never be broken. He is regarded by many as one of the toughest and grittiest quarterbacks in NFL history.

What would Manning himself say about these matters? Schooled by his father, and seasoned through years of disappointing playoff performances, he was usually tight-lipped about comparisons with other football greats. But those who watched him play in Super Bowl XLI got the sense that his competitive spirit has made him a great player. He wants to be the best, and if he stays healthy, he may well claim that title.

## PEYTON MANNING

**POSITION: Quarterback**

**FULL NAME:**
**Peyton Williams Manning**
**BORN: March 24, 1976,**
**New Orleans, Louisiana**
**HEIGHT: 6'5"**
**WEIGHT: 230 lbs.**

**COLLEGE:**
**Tennessee**
**TEAM:**
**Indianapolis**
**Colts (1998–**
**Present)**

| YEAR | TEAM | G | COMP | ATT | PCT | YD | Y/A | TD | INT |
|------|------|-----|------|------|------|--------|-----|-----|-----|
| 1998 | IND | 16 | 326 | 575 | 56.7 | 3,739 | 6.5 | 26 | 28 |
| 1999 | IND | 16 | 331 | 533 | 62.1 | 4,135 | 7.8 | 26 | 15 |
| 2000 | IND | 16 | 357 | 571 | 62.5 | 4,413 | 7.7 | 33 | 15 |
| 2001 | IND | 16 | 343 | 547 | 62.7 | 4,131 | 7.6 | 26 | 23 |
| 2002 | IND | 16 | 392 | 591 | 66.3 | 4,200 | 7.1 | 27 | 19 |
| 2003 | IND | 16 | 379 | 566 | 67.0 | 4,267 | 7.5 | 29 | 10 |
| 2004 | IND | 16 | 336 | 497 | 67.6 | 4,557 | 9.2 | 49 | 10 |
| 2005 | IND | 16 | 305 | 453 | 67.3 | 3,747 | 8.3 | 28 | 10 |
| 2006 | IND | 16 | 362 | 557 | 65.0 | 4,397 | 7.9 | 31 | 9 |
| 2007 | IND | 16 | 337 | 515 | 65.4 | 4,040 | 7.8 | 31 | 14 |
| **TOTALS** | | **160** | **3,468** | **5,405** | **64.2** | **41,626** | **7.7** | **306** | **153** |

# CHRONOLOGY

**1949**  Archie Manning born in Drew, Mississippi.

**1971**  Archie Manning marries Olivia Williams.

**1974**  Cooper Manning born.

**1976**  Peyton Manning born.

**1980**  Archie's worst year (1–15) with the New Orleans Saints.

**1981**  Eli Manning born.

**1982**  Archie Manning traded to Houston Oilers.

**1983**  Archie Manning traded to Minnesota Vikings.

**1984**  Archie retires from the NFL.

**1992**  Cooper Manning graduates from Newman High School.

**1993**  Cooper is sidelined, for good, with a congenital condition.

**1994**  Peyton Manning graduates from Newman High School; he is named Gatorade National Player of the Year after throwing for 39 touchdowns in his senior season; he enters the University of Tennessee.

**1997**  Manning decides to return for his senior year at Tennessee; he leaves Tennessee with 33 school records, eight SEC records, and two NCAA records.

**1998**  Manning drafted by the Indianapolis Colts; he signs a six-year, $48 million contract, which includes an $11.6 million signing bonus; the team goes 3–13 his first year, but Manning sets several NFL rookie records.

**1999**  Colts go 13–3 in Manning's second year—the best single-season turnaround in NFL history; team loses to the Tennessee Titans, 19-16, in divisional round of playoffs.

2000    Colts go 10–6 in Manning's third year; team loses to the Miami Dolphins, 23-17, in wild-card round of playoffs; brother Eli becomes starting quarterback at Ole Miss.

2001    Colts go 6–10 in Manning's fourth year; he misses one snap because of a broken jaw.

2002    Colts go 10–6 in the newly created AFC South Division; team loses to the New York Jets, 41-0, in wild-card round of playoffs.

2003    Colts go 12–4 in the AFC South Division; Manning and the Colts win a spectacular Monday Night Football game against Tampa Bay; team wins its first playoff game under Manning, defeating the Denver Broncos,

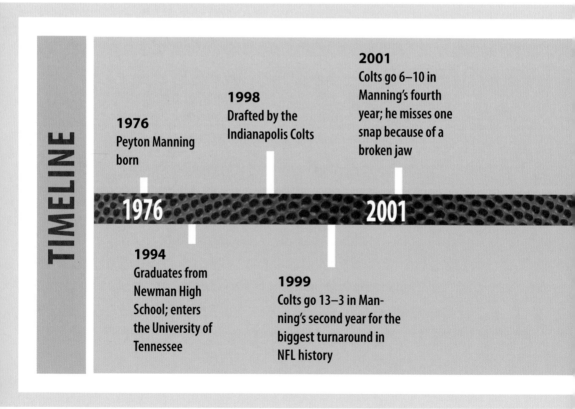

**TIMELINE**

**1976**
Peyton Manning born

**1998**
Drafted by the Indianapolis Colts

**2001**
Colts go 6–10 in Manning's fourth year; he misses one snap because of a broken jaw

1976                                              2001

**1994**
Graduates from Newman High School; enters the University of Tennessee

**1999**
Colts go 13–3 in Manning's second year for the biggest turnaround in NFL history

41-10, in the wild-card round of playoffs but lose to the Patriots in the AFC Championship Game, 24-14.

2004    Colts go 12–4; Manning plays his one hundredth game without missing a start; he breaks all-time touchdown record for one season with 49; after beating the Broncos, 49-24, for the second straight year in the wild-card round of the playoffs, the Colts again fall to the Patriots, this time in the divisional round, 20-3; Eli Manning is drafted by the New York Giants.

2005    Colts start season 13–0 and finish 14–2, even beating their nemesis, the New England Patriots during the regular season, but team falls to the Pittsburgh Steelers,

**2004**
Manning breaks all-time touchdown record for one season

**2006**
Peyton and Eli square off in first game of the season—first time in NFL history brothers face each other as starting quarterbacks

**2003**

**2007**

**2003**
Colts go 12–4 in the AFC South and advance to AFC Championship Game

**2005**
Colts start season 13–0 and finish 14–2 but are upset in divisional round of the playoffs

**2007**
Colts beat Chicago Bears in Super Bowl XLI, 29-17

PEYTON MANNING

21-18, in divisional round of playoffs; Tony Dungy's son James commits suicide.

2006    Peyton and Eli face each other for the first time in their careers, with Peyton coming out on top, 26-21.

2007    Manning and the Colts defeat Patriots, 38-34, to win AFC Championship; Colts beat Chicago Bears, 29-17, in Super Bowl XLI; Manning meets President Bush at White House; Manning and Carrie Underwood host *Saturday Night Live*.

# GLOSSARY

**American Football Conference (AFC)**   One of the two conferences in the National Football League (NFL). The AFC was established after the NFL merged with the American Football League (AFL) in 1970.

**audible**   A play called by the quarterback at the line of scrimmage to change the play that was called in the huddle.

**backup**   A second-string player who does not start the game, but comes in later in relief of a starter.

**blitz**   A defensive maneuver in which one or more linebackers or defensive backs, who normally remain behind the line of scrimmage, instead charge into the opponent's backfield.

**blocking**   When a player obstructs another player's path with his body. Examples: cut block, zone block, trap block, pull block, screen block, pass block, double-team block.

**bootleg**   An offensive play predicated upon misdirection in which the quarterback pretends to hand the ball to another player and then carries the ball in the opposite direction of the supposed ballcarrier with the intent of either passing or running (sometimes the quarterback has the option of doing either).

**center**   A player position on offense. The center snaps the ball.

**chain**   The 10-yard-long chain that is used by the chain crew (aka, "chain gang") to measure for a new series of downs.

**completion percentage** (*also* **pass completion rate**)   The percentage of passes thrown by a player that are completed. For example, if a running back throws one pass all season and completes it, his completion percentage would be 100 percent.

**cornerback**   A defensive back who lines up near the line of scrimmage across from a wide receiver. His primary job is to disrupt passing routes and to defend against short and medium passes in the passing game and to contain the rusher on running plays.

**defensive back**     A cornerback or safety position on the defensive team; commonly defends against wide receivers on passing plays. Generally there are four defensive backs playing at a time.

**defensive end**     A player position on defense who lines up on the outside of the defensive line whose principal function is to deliver pressure to the quarterback.

**defensive tackle**     A player position on defense on the inside of the defensive line whose principal function is to contain the run.

**drive**     A continuous set of offensive plays gaining substantial yardage and several first downs, usually leading to a scoring opportunity.

**end zone**     The area between the end line and the goal line, bounded by the sidelines.

**extra point**     A single point scored in a conversion attempt after a touchdown by place- or drop-kicking the ball through the opponent's goal.

**field goal**     Score of three points made by place- or drop-kicking the ball through the opponent's goal.

**first down**     The first of a set of four downs. Usually, a team that has a first down needs to advance the ball 10 yards to receive another first down, but penalties or field position (i.e., less than 10 yards from the opposing end zone) can affect this.

**formation**     An arrangement of the offensive skill players.

**fourth down**     The final of a set of four downs. Unless a first down is achieved or a penalty forces a replay of the down, the team will lose control of the ball after this play. If a team does not think they can get a first down, they often punt on fourth down or kick a field goal if they are close enough to do so.

**fullback**     A player position on offense. In modern formations, this position may be varied, and this player has more blocking responsibilities in comparison to the halfback or tailback.

**fumble**     A ball that a player accidentally loses possession of.

**goal line**    The front of the end zone.

**guard**    One of two player positions on offense (linemen).

**handoff**    A player's handing of a live ball to another player. The handoff goes either backwards or laterally, as opposed to a forward pass.

**holding**    There are two kinds of holding: offensive holding, illegally blocking a player from the opposing team by grabbing and holding his uniform or body; and defensive holding, called against defensive players who impede receivers who are more than five yards from the line of scrimmage, but who are not actively making an attempt to catch the ball.

**huddle**    An on-field gathering of members of a team in order to secretly communicate instructions for the upcoming play.

**incomplete pass**    A forward pass of the ball that no player legally caught.

**interception**    The legal catching of a forward pass thrown by an opposing player.

**kickoff**    A free kick that starts each half, or restarts the game following a touchdown or field goal.

**line of scrimmage/scrimmage line**    One of two vertical planes parallel to the goal line when the ball is to be put in play by scrimmage.

**linebacker**    A player position on defense. The linebackers typically play one to six yards behind the defensive linemen and are the most versatile players on the field because they can play both run and pass defense or are called to blitz.

**man-to-man coverage**    A defense in which all players in pass coverage, typically linebackers and defensive backs, cover a specific player.

**National Collegiate Athletic Association (NCAA)**    Principal governing body of college sports, including college football.

**National Football Conference (NFC)**    One of the two conferences in the National Football League (NFL). The NFC was established after the NFL merged with the American Football League (AFL) in 1970.

**National Football League (NFL)**    The largest professional American football league, with 32 teams.

**offside**    An infraction of the rule that requires both teams to be on their own side of their restraining line as or before the ball is put in play. Offside is typically called on the defensive team.

**option**    A type of play in which the quarterback has the option of handing off, keeping, or laterally passing to one or more backs. Often described by a type of formation or play action, such as triple option, veer option, or counter option.

**pass interference**    When a player illegally hinders an eligible receiver's opportunity to catch a forward pass.

**passer rating** (*also* **quarterback rating**)    A numeric value used to measure the performance of quarterbacks. It was formulated in 1973 and it uses the player's completion percentage, passing yards, touchdowns, and interceptions.

**play action**    A tactic in which the quarterback fakes either a handoff or a throw in order to draw the defense away from the intended offensive method.

**pocket**    An area on the offensive side of the line of scrimmage, where the offensive linemen attempt to prevent the defensive players from reaching the quarterback during passing plays.

**position**    A place where a player plays relative to teammates, and/or a role filled by that player.

**punt**    A kick in which the ball is dropped and kicked before it reaches the ground; used to give up the ball to the opposition after offensive downs have been used.

**quarterback**    An offensive player who lines up behind the center, from whom he takes the snap.

**reception**    When a player catches (receives) the ball.

**running back**    A player position on offense. Although the term usually refers to the halfback or tailback, fullbacks are also considered running backs.

**sack**    Tackling a ballcarrier who intends to throw a forward pass. A sack also is awarded if a player forces a fumble of the ball, or the ballcarrier to go out of bounds, behind the line of scrimmage on an apparent intended forward pass play.

**safety**    A player position on defense; a method of scoring (worth two points) by downing an opposing ballcarrier in his own end zone, forcing the opposing ballcarrier out of his own end zone and out of bounds, or forcing the offensive team to fumble the ball so that it exits the end zone.

**salary cap**    A limit on the amount any NFL team can spend on its players' salaries; the salary cap was introduced in 1994 in order to bring parity to the NFL.

**scramble**    On a called passing play, when the quarterback runs from the pocket in an attempt to avoid being sacked, giving the receivers more time to get open or attempting to gain positive yards by running himself.

**secondary**    Refers to the defensive "backfield," specifically the safeties and cornerbacks.

**shotgun formation**    Formation in which offensive team may line up at the start of a play. In this formation, the quarterback receives the snap five to eight yards behind the center.

**sideline**    One of the lines marking each side of the field.

**snap**    The handoff or pass from the center that begins a play from scrimmage.

**special teams**    The units that handle kickoffs, punts, free kicks, and field-goal attempts.

**starter**    A player who is the first to play his position within a given game or season. Depending on the position and the game situation, this player may be replaced or share time with one or more players later in the game. For example, a quarterback may start the game but be replaced by a backup quarterback if the game becomes one-sided.

**tackle**   The act of forcing a ballcarrier to the ground. Also a position on the offensive/defensive line.

**tailback**   Player position on offense farthest ("deepest") back, except in kicking formations.

**tight end**   A player position on offense—often known as a Y receiver when he lines up on the line of scrimmage—next to the offensive tackle. Tight ends are used as blockers during running plays and either run a route or stay in to block during passing plays.

**time of possession**   The amount of time one team has the ball in its possession relative to the other team.

**touchdown**   A play worth six points, accomplished by gaining legal possession of the ball in the opponent's end zone. It also allows the team a chance for one extra point by kicking the ball or a chance to attempt a two-point conversion.

**turnover**   The loss of the ball by one team to the other team. This is usually the result of a fumble or an interception.

**wide receiver**   A player position on offense. He is split wide (usually about 10 yards) from the formation and plays on the line of scrimmage as a split end (X) or one yard off as a flanker (Z).

**wild card**   The two playoff spots given to the two nondivision-winning teams that have the best records in each conference.

**wishbone**   A formation involving three running backs lined up behind the quarterback in the shape of a Y, similar to the shape of a wishbone.

**yard**   One yard of linear distance in the direction of one of the two goals. A field is 100 yards. Typically, a team is required to advance at least 10 yards in order to get a new set of downs.

**zone defense**   A defense in which players who are in pass coverage cover zones of the field, instead of individual players.

# BIBLIOGRAPHY

Chappell, Mike, and Phil Richards. *Tales from the Indianapolis Colts Sideline*. Champaign, Ill.: Sports Publishing, 2004.

Ernsberger, Richard, Jr. *Bragging Rights: A Season Inside the SEC, College Football's Toughest Conference*. New York: M. Evans and Company, 2000.

Halberstam, David. *The Education of a Coach*. New York: Hyperion, 2005.

Hyams, Jimmy. *Peyton Manning: Primed and Ready*. Kansas City: Addax Publishing Group, 1998.

MacCambridge, Michael, ed. *ESPN College Football Encyclopedia: The Complete History of the Game*. Bristol, Conn.: ESPN, 2006.

———. *America's Game: The Epic Story of How Pro Football Captured a Nation*. New York: Random House, 2004.

Manning, Archie, and Peyton, with John Underwood. *Manning*. New York: Harper Collins, 2001.

Palmer, Peter, Ken Pullis, Sean Lahman, Matthew Silverman, Gary Gillette, eds. *The ESPN Pro Football Encyclopedia*. New York: Sterling Publishing, 2006.

Pierce, Charles P. *Moving the Chains: Tom Brady and the Pursuit of Everything*. New York: Farrar, Straus and Giroux, 2006.

Serpas, Christian. *The New Orleans Saints: 25 Years of Heroic Effort*. Lafayette, La.: Acadian House Publishing, 1991.

*True Blue: The Colts' Unforgettable 2006 Championship Season*. Chicago: Triumph Books, 2007.

# FURTHER READING

Chappell, Mike, and Phil Richards. *Tales from the Indianapolis Colts Sideline*. Champaign, Ill.: Sports Publishing, 2004.

Griffith, Mike, and Nathan Kirkham. *Game Day Tennessee Football: The Greatest Games, Players, Coaches and Teams in the Glorious Tradition of Volunteer Football*. Chicago: Triumph Books, 2006.

Hyams, Jimmy. *Peyton Manning: Primed and Ready*. Kansas City: Addax Publishing Group, 1998.

Pierce, Charles P. *Moving the Chains: Tom Brady and the Pursuit of Everything*. New York: Farrar, Straus and Giroux, 2006.

*True Blue: The Colts' Unforgettable 2006 Championship Season*. Chicago: Triumph Books, 2007.

## WEB SITES

### Indianapolis Star (Indianapolis Colts)
http://www.indystar.com/apps/pbcs.dll/section?Category=SPORTS03

### Peyton Manning's Official Web site
http://peytonmanning.com

### The Tennessean: Roundup of University of Tennessee Sports
http://www.tennessean.com

# PICTURE CREDITS

# INDEX